AMERICA
TO PRAY?
⸺ OR ⸺
NOT TO PRAY?

David Barton

WallBuilder Press
P.O. Box 397
Aledo, Texas 76008
817-441-6044

Printed in the United States of America
ISBN 0-925279-42-0

Cover Photo: Courtesy of the Supreme Court of the United States

Preface

In July 1987, God impressed me to do two things; His leading seemed so "non-spiritual" that I questioned it, but the two impressions were so strong that I could not ignore them. First, I was to find the date that prayer had first been prohibited in public schools. Second, I was to obtain a record of national SAT scores (the academic test given to prospective college-bound high-school students) spanning the last several decades.

I had believed that the two instructions were separate and distinct, yet I soon discovered that they were unquestionably related. I obtained the SAT scores and noticed that while the scores had been relatively stable from 1952-1962, after 1963 their decline had been so rapid that it appeared they were tumbling down a steep mountainside. Next, I learned that corporate verbal prayer had been removed from schools and forbidden to public school students in two Court decisions in 1962-63.

When I superimposed the two items, I was astounded (see the chart on the following page). I thought to myself, "Can it really be possible that prayer was removed in '62 and academics began to decline in '63?" But the correlation was clear. I felt I was now armed with some fascinating statistical information; I just didn't know what to do with it!

That fall, I had opportunity to present the two pieces of information to a U. S. Congressman. He, too, was amazed at the apparent correlation. He informed me that, to his knowledge, in all the Congressional controversy surrounding the attempt to return religious principles to schools, statistical information had never been presented. School prayer had always previously been considered a "religious" issue only; this was the first time in his extended tenure in Congress that he had seen information suggesting any tangible effect of religious principles in schools. He stared at the chart, shook his head, and declared, "Someone ought to research this!"

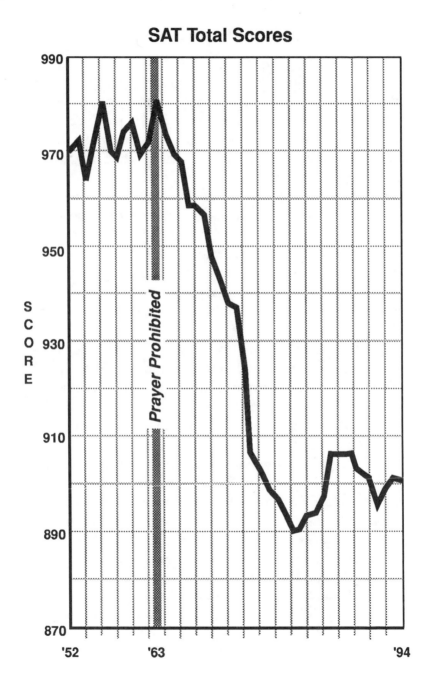

SAT Total Scores

Although the Congressman had voiced the words, the effect was the same as if God Himself had personally delivered my commission.

After I returned home, God outlined the strategy for pursuing further research through a comment made by our secretary. She had been examining the simple 22-word prayer from the *Engel* v. *Vitale* case (the 1962 case the Court first used to negate school prayer):

> *Almighty God, we acknowledge our dependence upon Thee, and we beg Thy blessings upon us, our parents, our teachers, and our Country.*

As we were discussing how the removal of such a simple prayer might have so profoundly affected the SAT scores, she observed that probably all four of the areas mentioned in the students' prayer (students, families, schools, and the nation) had declined dramatically since 1962. Even though she voiced the words, the effect on me was the same as it had been at the Congressman's office—it was as if God had again clearly spoken to my heart.

My curiosity was stirred. Had the change in national policy—the separation of religious principles from public affairs—resulted in any measurable difference for young people, their families, their schools, and their nation?

I began a long, arduous search of statistical information, information obtained primarily from federal cabinet level agencies (Departments of Health and Human Services, Justice, Education, Labor, Commerce, etc.). With the aid of dedicated co-workers, we searched through literally thousands of articles and documents relating to the four areas. The results of that search, as will be evident, are both clear and shocking.

While in 1988 I initially saw the removal of school prayer as the cause for the decline, I now know that there was much more involved. As the courts have explained in no less than ten different cases:

> Prayer is the quintessential religious practice. [1]

Prayer, an acknowledgment of God, is the simplest identification of a philosophy which recognizes not only the God of heaven but also His laws and standards of conduct. Prayer, the "heart" of religion, was by necessity the first target of a general attack on all religious principles. After the removal of prayer, there quickly followed cases rejecting not only the Bible but any values derived from them (the Ten Commandments, the teaching of pre-marital sexual abstinence to students, etc.).

The removal of prayer was the first step on the infamous "slippery slope." While the removal of school prayer cannot be blamed for all the declines, the presence or absence, legality or illegality, of prayer and the acknowledgment of God in public arenas is the primary indicator of the philosophy under which official public policy is being conducted. When there is an official recognition of prayer—"the quintessential religious practice"—there is also an embracing of the values and teachings of which prayer is a primary indicator.

For this reason, the return of school prayer is essential—as you will soon see on the subsequent pages. The return of school prayer will be a signal that the first step has been taken not only toward recognizing God, but toward reinstating His system upon which our traditional moral, ethical, and disciplinary standards depend.

David Barton
September, 1994

America:
To Pray Or Not To Pray?

Table of Contents

Index to Charts, Tables, and Graphs

Chapter 1
An Historical Overview

The heritage of this nation is undeniably religious. Beginning with the first explorers and moving on to the Pilgrims, the American Revolution, the Civil War, and even long after, religion had a strong, positive influence on the successful development of this nation. As explained in *Compton's Encyclopedia:*

> The most powerful single influence in all history has been Christianity. This influence has shown itself not only in the religious beliefs and spiritual ideals of the human race, but in the march of political events and institutions as well. [1]

We are surrounded with recognitions of religion's positive influence on our nation: our National Anthem reflects our reliance on God; our money declares our faith in God; and our Pledge of Allegiance heralds our testimony to God's importance in this nation. Supreme Court decisions have affirmed the religious faith of this nation:

> In 1892 the United States Supreme Court made an exhaustive study of the supposed connection between Christianity and the government of the United States. After reviewing hundreds of volumes of historical documents, the Court asserted, "These references ... add a volume of unofficial declarations to the mass of organic utterances that this is a religious people ... a Christian nation." Likewise, in 1931 Supreme Court Justice George Sutherland reviewed the 1892 decision in reference to another case and reiterated that Americans are a "Christian people." And in 1952 Justice William O. Douglas affirmed that "we are a religious people and our institutions presuppose a Supreme Being." [2]

One of the arenas in which religion was most visible was in American public education. Our nation's first schools were in churches, and for more than three centuries following their inception in the mid-1600s, public schools promoted prayer and regularly used the Bible as a textbook; traditional religious principles was the basis for teaching morals and stories drawn from those principles often provided the content for student readers. Students trained in these public schools were well-rounded and well-equipped, educated both in mind and in character. Noah Webster, a Founding Father and leading educator, accurately reflected the nation's beliefs when he stated:

> No truth is more evident to my mind than that the Christian religion must be the basis of any government intended to secure the rights and privileges of a free people. [3]

Benjamin Rush, a signer of the Declaration of Independence and the first Founder to call for free public schools, similarly explained:

> [T]he only foundation for a useful education in a republic is to be laid in religion. Without this there can be no virtue, and without virtue there can be no liberty, and liberty is the object and life of all republican governments. . . . [4]
> Without religion, I believe learning does much mischief to the morals and principles of mankind. [5]

From its inception, our nation had believed in the power and the results of religious teachings and practices and had strongly supported their inclusion in public arenas. Revered national political leaders believed that public prayer could and would change the course of the nation. For example, consider Benjamin Franklin's lengthy speech delivered at the Constitutional Convention. The nation's elder statesman and patriarch (and today considered to be one of the least religious of the Founding Fathers) reminded the other delegates:

> In the beginning of the contest with Britain, when we were sensible of danger, we had daily prayers in this room for Divine protection. Our prayers, Sir, were heard, and they were graciously answered. All of us who were engaged in the struggle must have observed frequent instances of a superintending Providence in our favor. . . . And have we now forgotten this powerful Friend? Or do we imagine we

no longer need His assistance? I have lived, Sir, a long time, and the longer I live, the more convincing proofs I see of this truth: "that God governs in the affairs of man." And if a sparrow cannot fall to the ground without His notice, is it probable that an empire can rise without His aid? We have been assured, Sir, in the Sacred Writings that except the Lord build the house, they labor in vain that build it. I firmly believe this. I also believe that without His concurring aid, we shall succeed in the political building no better than the builders of Babel; we shall be divided by our little, partial local interests; our projects will be confounded; and we ourselves shall become a reproach and a byword down to future ages. And what is worse, mankind may hereafter from this unfortunate instance, despair of establishing government by human wisdom and leave it to chance, war, or conquest. I therefore beg leave to move that, henceforth, prayers imploring the assistance of Heaven and its blessing on our deliberation be held in this assembly every morning before we proceed to business. [6]

As Franklin noted, God had often answered their prayers and manifested Himself throughout the struggle with Great Britain; He blessed their efforts at the Constitutional Convention no less—a fact noted by many of the Founders, including Benjamin Rush:

I do not believe that the Constitution was the offspring of inspiration, but I am as perfectly satisfied that the Union of the States in its form and adoption is as much the work of a Divine Providence as any of the miracles recorded in the Old and New Testament. [7]

George Washington was another of the many Founding Fathers who avidly believed in the importance of prayer. Numerous paintings show "The Father of Our Country" in prayer, including the stained glass window in the U. S. Congressional Chapel and the monument at Valley Forge. Even his first speech after his election as President was marked by his call for prayer:

It would be peculiarly improper to omit, in this first official act, my fervent supplication to that Almighty Being who rules over the universe, who presides in the councils of nations, and whose providential aids can supply every human defect.... No people can be bound to acknowledge and adore the invisible hand which conducts the affairs of men more than the people of the United States. [8]

He then warned:

[T]he propitious [favorable] smiles of Heaven can never be expected on a nation that disregards the eternal rules of order and right which Heaven itself has ordained. [9]

For eight years, Washington wisely and skillfully guided this nation to a position from which its continued strength and development would be assured. In his "Farewell Address," he warned:

Of all the dispositions and habits which lead to political prosperity, religion and morality are indispensable supports. In vain would that man claim the tribute of patriotism who should labour to subvert these great pillars of human happiness.... The mere politician, equally with the pious man, ought to respect and to cherish them. [10]

Franklin had warned that "forgetting God" and imagining that we no longer needed His "concurring aid" would result in internal disputes, the decay of the nation's prestige and reputation, and a diminished national success. Washington had warned that if religious principles were excluded, the nation's morality and political prosperity would suffer. Yet, despite such clear words, in cases beginning in 1962, the Supreme Court offered rulings which eventually divorced the nation, its schools, and its public affairs from more than three centuries of its heritage; America is now learning experientially what both Washington and Franklin knew to be true; we are suffering in the very areas they predicted.

Chapter 2
1962—A New Direction For America

In decisions rendered on June 25, 1962, in *Engel* v. *Vitale*, and on June 17, 1963, in *Murray* v. *Curlett* and *Abington* v. *Schempp*, the Supreme Court forbade the inclusion of religious activities in major activities of daily student life by striking down school prayer and Bible reading. Never before in the history of our nation had any branch of our government taken such a stand.

Through those decisions, thirty-nine million students and over two million teachers were barred from participating in what had been available to students since our nation's founding. Even today, millions of Americans personally recall when prayer, Bible reading, and religious principles were as much a part of their public school activities as was the study of math or the pursuit of athletics. Activities once considered an integral part of education are now totally censured.

This sudden and dramatic restructuring of educational policies was precipitated by the Court's reinterpretation of the phrase "separation of church and state." The First Amendment does not contain that phrase; it simply states, "Congress shall make no law respecting an establishment of religion, or prohibiting the free exercise thereof." This had always meant that Congress was prohibited from establishing a national religious denomination—that Congress could not pass a law requiring Americans to become Catholics, Anglicans, or members of any other denomination.

This meaning for "separation of church and state" had been explained clearly during the time of the Founders and was applied by the Courts for 170 years afterwards. But, in 1962, the Supreme Court decided that "church" would no longer mean a "federal denomination"; instead, it would now mean a "religious activity in public." Consequently, "separation of church and state" was no longer a prohibition against establishing a national denomination; it was now a prohibition against including religious activities in public affairs.

This new interpretation of "church" immediately invited hundreds of lawsuits challenging any presence of religion in public life. While skyrocketing numbers of lawsuits are still awaiting disposition, courts[†] have already delivered far-reaching decisions to:

- *Remove student prayer:* "Prayer in its public school system breaches the constitutional wall of separation between Church and State." ENGEL v. VITALE, 1962 [1]

- *Remove school Bible readings:* "[N]o state law or school board may require that passages from the Bible be read or that the Lord's Prayer be recited in the public schools of a State at the beginning of each school day." ABINGTON v. SCHEMPP, 1963 [2]

- *Remove the Ten Commandments from view:* "If the posted copies of the Ten Commandments are to have any effect at all, it will be to induce the schoolchildren to read, meditate upon, perhaps to venerate and obey, the Commandments . . . this . . . is not a permissible state objective under the Establishment Clause." STONE v. GRAHAM, 1980 [3]

- *Remove benedictions and invocations from school activities:* "Religious invocation . . . in high school commencement exercise conveyed message that district had given its endorsement to prayer and religion, so that school district was properly [prohibited] from including invocation in commencement exercise." GRAHAM v. CENTRAL, 1985; [4] KAY v. DOUGLAS, 1986; [5] JAGER v. DOUGLAS, 1989; [6] LEE v. WEISMAN, 1992 [7]

---

† A note about the difference in usage between "Court" and "court" should be made. "Court" (capital "C") refers to the Supreme Court of the United States, whereas "court" (lower-case "c") indicates a State Supreme Court or any other court, whether federal or state. Similarly, "Courts" specifically refers to the decisions of collective U. S. Supreme Courts and "courts" refers to the judiciary in general, represented by its jurisdiction from the lowest level local courts through the Supreme Court of the United States.

Lower court rulings have gone even further than those of the Supreme Court, chipping away at the original intent until a religion-hostile attitude is now the norm in many courts. Today, there is such an anti-religious prejudice in education that some courts have forbidden the following activities within their jurisdiction:

- Freedom of speech and press is guaranteed to students unless the topic is religious, at which time such speech becomes unconstitutional. STEIN v. OSHINSKY, 1965; [8] COLLINS v. CHANDLER UNIFIED SCHOOL DISTRICT., 1981 [9]

- If a student prays over his lunch, it is unconstitutional for him to pray aloud. REED v. VAN HOVEN, 1965 [10]

- It is unconstitutional for a Board of Education to use or refer to the word "God" in any of its official writings. OHIO v. WHISNER, 1976 [11]

Many state and local officials have gone even further than these courts. For example:

- Public schools were barred from showing a film about the settlement of Jamestown because the film depicted the erection of a cross at the settlement, despite the historical fact that a cross was erected at the Jamestown settlement. [12]

- In the Alaska public schools, students were told they could not use the word "Christmas" in school because it had the word "Christ" in it, nor could they have the word in their notebooks, nor exchange Christmas cards or presents, nor display anything with the word "Christmas" on it. [13]

- In Colorado, a music teacher was stopped from singing traditional Christmas carols in her classes. [14]

These rulings are not without consequence; what occurs in the classroom eventually affects the rest of the nation. As explained by President Abraham Lincoln:

The philosophy of the class room in one generation will
be the philosophy of government in the next. [15]

The current anti-religious bias in education is new, having been
implemented only after the redefinition of the First Amendment in
1962. Only eight years later, the Court acknowledged that it had
begun a legal revolution, even admitting that:

> It was . . . not until 1962 that . . . prayers were held to
> violate the [First Amendment]. [16]

The Court further conceded that the decision to remove prayer
had been made without *any* previous precedent, either legal or historical. However, the Court argued that it needed no precedent:

> Finally, in *Engel* v. *Vitale*, only last year, these principles
> [the separation of prayer from the classroom] were so
> *universally recognized* that the Court, ***without the citation
> of a single case*** . . . reaffirmed them. [17]

The Court attempted to invoke peer pressure to justify its lack of
precedent: i.e., "everyone" understands the removal of prayer was necessary. However, the so-called "universally recognized" principles calling
for the separation of religious principles from public education were
so foreign that many commented on the new and dramatic change.
For example, the *1963 World Book Encyclopedia Yearbook* stated:

> The significance of the decision regarding this [school]
> prayer was enormous, for the whole thorny problem of
> religion in public education *was thus inevitably raised.* [18]

Notice that prior to this case, the legal issue of separating prayer
and religious principles from education had not been "raised." Legal
observers also commented on the Court's departure from precedent:

> The Court has broken *new ground* in a number of fields.
> . . . Few Supreme Court decisions of recent years have
> created greater furor than *Engel* v. *Vitale*. [19]

Few professionals agreed with the Court that its decisions were based on "universally recognized" principles. In fact, in *Zorach* v. *Clauson*, only ten short years before, the Court was still embracing the philosophy it had maintained for over a century-and-a-half, declaring:

> The First Amendment, however, does *not* say that in every and all respects there shall be a separation of Church and State. . . . Otherwise the state and religion would be aliens to each other—hostile, suspicious, and even unfriendly. [20]

How could the 1962 Supreme Court Justices so quickly repudiate nearly two centuries of Supreme Court rulings? How could they have ignored the Court's lengthy history of protecting Christian principles and religious activities in public education? Perhaps the answer rests in the fact that eight of the nine Justices on the 1962-63 Supreme Court had been appointed to the Court following an extended history of political rather than judicial experience.

For example, Chief Justice Earl Warren had been the Governor of California for ten years prior to his appointment; Justice Hugo Black had been a U. S. Senator for ten years; Justice Felix Frankfurter had been an assistant to the Secretary of Labor and a founding member of the ACLU; Justice Arthur Goldberg had been the Secretary of Labor; Justice William Douglas was chairman of the Securities and Exchange Commission prior to his appointment. All of the Justices except one had similar political backgrounds.

Justice Potter Stewart, a federal judge for four years prior to his appointment, was the *only* member of the Court with extended federal Constitutional experience prior to his appointment. Interestingly, he was also the *only* Justice who objected to the removal of prayer and Bible reading. He alone acted as a judge; the rest acted as politicians, determined to develop new policies rather than to uphold previous precedents.

Those activist Justices not only initiated the Christian hostile policy, they firmly guided and strengthened it during their tenure. However, their anti-religious rulings were by no means limited solely to education; they also caused the reversal of long-standing social policies for children, families, and the nation. In fact, each of these arenas had preserved an extended legal history during which the Court had not only refused to exclude religious principles, but had relied upon them when rendering its decisions. The following statements are representative of those which appeared in scores of cases:

> Christianity has reference to the principles of right and wrong . . . it is the foundation of those morals and manners upon which our society is formed; it is their basis. Remove this and they would fall . . . [Morality] has grown upon the basis of Christianity. . . . The day of moral virtue in which we live would, in an instant, if that standard were abolished, lapse into the dark and murky night of pagan immorality. CHARLESTON v. BENJAMIN [21]

> The morality of the country is deeply engrafted upon Christianity . . . [We are] people whose manners . . . and whose morals have been elevated and inspired . . . by means of the Christian religion. PEOPLE v. RUGGLES [22]

The subsequent chapters will present clear and compelling evidence of the extensive damage caused to many aspects of national life by the separation of Biblical principles from public affairs and national policy in 1962-63.

Let it be stressed that the removal of school prayer was *not* the culprit for all of the nation's ills; an instant return of school prayer will *not* provide an instantaneous cure. The rejection of school prayer simply indicated the introduction of a new national policy which was religion-hostile.

School prayer was the simplest identification of a philosophy recognizing not only the God of heaven, but also His laws and standards of conduct as well. For example, where prayer is found, it is not surprising also to find the Bible, the Ten Commandments, traditional moral teachings, etc. Conversely, where there is an absence of prayer, it is not surprising that there is also an absence of Biblical principles or traditional values. In fact, it would be surprising to find religious values present where prayer is absent. As the Court first noted in *Jaffree* v. *Wallace* (and in nine other cases to date):

Prayer is the quintessential religious practice. [23]

The removal of school prayer was simply the first visible manifestation of a war on all public religious expression; it provided the judicial "toehold" needed to accomplish the subsequent extraction of other beliefs and practices rooted in religious teachings which had long been held as fundamental to national behavior and thus national policy.

The simple prayer struck down by the Court in 1962 will serve as the basic outline for this book:

Almighty God, we acknowledge our dependence upon Thee, and we beg Thy blessings upon us, our parents, our teachers, and our Country. [24]

The categories of *"us"* (the students), *"our parents"* (the families), *"our teachers"* (the academic leaders), and *"our Country"* (the nation) identifies the four major areas examined in this work. Through the use of statistical information gathered primarily from U. S. government offices, the years when religious and moral principles guided our national policies in each of these areas will be contrasted with the years following their rejection.

Chapter 3
"Us"—The Youth

George Washington, in his "Farewell Address," warned:

> And let us with caution indulge the supposition that morality may be maintained without religion. Whatever may be conceded to the influence of refined education on minds . . . reason and experience both forbid us to expect that national morality can prevail in exclusion of religious principle. [1]

Washington's statement was not a radical new teaching; it was the articulation of a fundamental belief widely held among the Founders. Not only reason but also experience had proved that morality could not be maintained without religious principles.

Yet today, so completely have religious principles been expunged from education that a court even ruled *against* a traditional moral teaching for students in public schools (premarital sexual abstinence) because that teaching had religious roots. The court explained:

> The harm of premarital sexual relations . . . [is] elements of religious doctrine. It is a fundamental tenet of many religions that premarital sex . . . [is] wrong. . . . In short, [teaching pre-marital sexual abstinence] has the primary effect of advancing religion. This alone would force the court to declare the law constitutionally infirm. . . . [T]he inescapable conclusion is that federal funds have been used . . . to teach matters inherently tied to religion.
> KENDRICK v. BOWEN [2]

Although this case was eventually modified by the Supreme Court, the fact that it even reached the Court indicates the extent to which basic moral values have been rejected by many courts. In a similar vein, the state of California was recently considering adopting legislation on sex-education for public schools requiring that:

Course material and instruction shall stress that
monogamous heterosexual intercourse [one man and one
woman] within marriage is a traditional American value. [3]

However, the Senator promoting that bill received a strong letter
of protest from the ACLU:

It is our position that monogamous, heterosexual
intercourse within marriage as a traditional American value
is an unconstitutional establishment of a religious doctrine
in public schools. . . . We believe [this bill] violates the
First Amendment. [4]

With such legal opposition to the teaching of "religious" sexual
and moral behavior, school students across the nation now are provided with "non-religious" sex-education curriculum from groups like
Planned Parenthood. These materials typically contain photographs,
illustrations, and graphics not only encouraging but also demonstrating the ease of performing pre-marital sex. Consider these "mild"
and relatively "non-offensive" excerpts from materials such groups
recommend for adolescents:

Boys and Sex: [5]

More people are coming to understand that having sex is
a joyful and enriching experience *at any age.* (p. 2)

Playing with girls sexually *before adolescence* . . . increases
the chances for a satisfactory sex life when a boy grows
up. (p. 38)

*Premarital intercourse does have its definite values as a
training ground* for marriage . . . boys and girls who start
having intercourse when they're adolescents . . . will find
that it's a big help; . . . it's like taking a car out on a test
run before you buy it. (p. 117)

Girls and Sex: [6]

> Girls understand now that they are far more likely to make good social and sexual adjustments to life if they learn to be warm, open, responsive, and *sexually unafraid.* They're learning to be sexual partners of men. (pp. 10-11)

> Everyone's agreed ... that *teenage sex should be a learning experience.* (p. 15)

> *Sex play with boys ... can be exciting, pleasurable, and even worthwhile* ... it will help later sexual adjustment. (p. 48)

You've Changed the Combination: [7]

> There are only two basic kinds of sex: sex with victims and sex without. One way to avoid having victims is, of course, to *have sexual relationships only with your friends.*

The Great Orgasm Robbery: [8]

> Sex is fun, and joyful ... and it comes in all types and styles, all of which are OK. *Don't rob yourself of joy by focusing on old-fashioned ideas about what's "normal" or "nice."*

Previous courts never tolerated such teachings, as illustrated by this Supreme Court declaration:

> There have been sects which ... advocated promiscuous intercourse of the sexes as prompted by the passions of its members. ... Should such a sect ... ever find its way into this country, swift punishment would follow the carrying into effect of its doctrines and no heed would be given to the pretence that ... their supporters could be protected in their exercise by the Constitution of the United States.
> DAVIS v. BEASON [9]

The Court has now reversed its previous long-held position, and the effects of that reversal are apparent. Notice in the following graphs the unusually strong correlation between the removal of religious principles and the changes in student moral behavior:

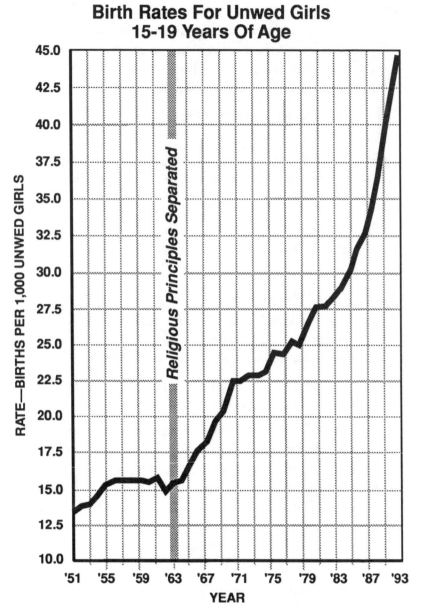

Birth Rates For Unwed Girls
15-19 Years Of Age

Basic data from Department of Health and Human Services and
Statistical Abstracts of the United States.

Pregnancies Among Unwed Girls Under 15 Years of Age

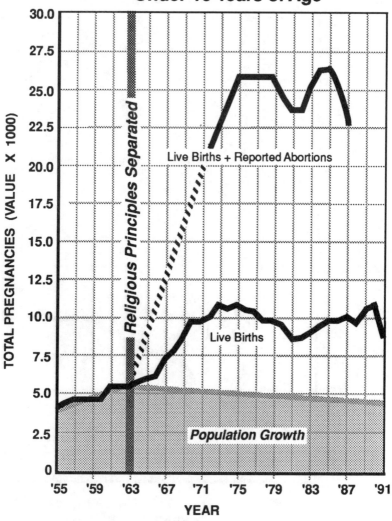

TOTAL PREGNANCIES (VALUE X 1000)

Live Births + Reported Abortions

Religious Principles Separated

Live Births

Population Growth

YEAR

Indicates population growth.
Indicates interpolated data.

Basic data from Department of Health and Human Services, *Statistical Abstracts of the United States*, the Center for Disease Control, and the Department of Commerce, Census Bureau.

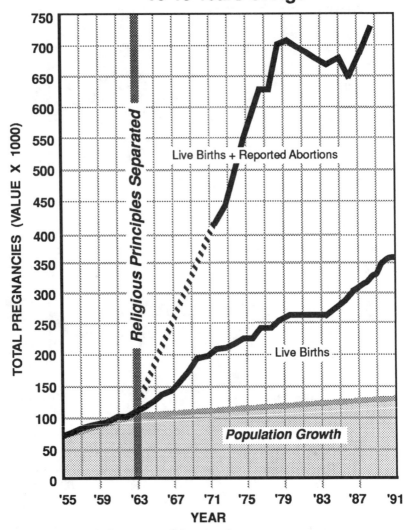

Pregnancies Among Unwed Girls 15-19 Years Of Age

Indicates population growth.
Indicates interpolated data.

Basic data from Department of Health and Human Services, *Statistical Abstracts of the United States,* the Center for Disease Control, and the Department of Commerce, Census Bureau.

Information on Teen Pregnancies

The overall effects of the moral changes go well beyond those indicated by the charts. For example:

- Teenage pregnancies have increased over 400 percent since 1962-63, [10] and the United States now has the highest incidence of teenage motherhood of any Western country. [11]

- By 1970, the percentage of out of wedlock births to teens had climbed to 29 percent, and by 1988 it had skyrocketed to 69 percent. [12]

- Each day, 2,756 teens become pregnant and 1,340 babies are born to teen mothers. [13]

- One-and-a-quarter million adolescent girls become pregnant each year, [14] and of those who give birth, half are not yet 18. [15]

- Of girls between the ages of 15 and 19, ten percent get pregnant each year, with 84 percent of the pregnancies being unwanted. [16]

- Currently, 80 percent of pregnant teenage girls are unmarried. [17]

- Teenage motherhood among school students is so prevalent that a Dallas high school established a 15-bed nursery for students with children, [18] and Houston has dedicated two entire high-schools for pregnant students. [19]

The economic impact of teen pregnancies is enormous:

- About 50 percent of all teen mothers are on welfare within one year of the birth of the first child; 77 percent join the welfare rolls within five years; and 43 percent of long-term welfare recipients started their families as unwed teens. [20]

- In 1985 alone, $16.65 billion was paid through welfare to women who gave birth as teenagers; [21] in 1990, the cost had risen to $21.55 billion. [22]

- Of those families headed by a mother age 14-25, two-thirds live below the poverty level. [23]
- Of the 1.3 million children of teenage mothers, 62 percent are currently in need of day care. [24]
- Of those who give birth before age 18, only half complete high school (compared with 96 percent for those who wait); they earn half as much money; and they are far more likely to end up on welfare. [25]

(Sexually Transmitted Diseases—STDs)

Changes in student morality are also evident in the measurements of sexually transmitted diseases:

- Cases of gonorrhea among junior-high students ages 10-14 have increased almost 400 percent since 1962-63. [26]
- As many as 40 percent of sexually-active teenage girls may be infected with the STD human papilloma virus (HPV) which causes genital warts. [27]
- Nine percent of female students are infected with the STD genital herpes. [28]
- Each year 4,000 students become infected with syphilis. [29]
- Up to 20 percent of AIDS victims were infected in their teens. [30]
- AIDS cases among teens have increased 62 percent since 1990, [31] and the number of teens with AIDS is doubling every 14 months. [32]
- AIDS is now the sixth leading cause of death among young adults. [33]
- Over three million teens, one in six sexually active teens, become infected each year with one of the more than two dozen STDs. [34]

The following graph illustrates what has become common with students and many STDs:

Sexually Transmitted Diseases
Gonorrhea: Age Group 10-14

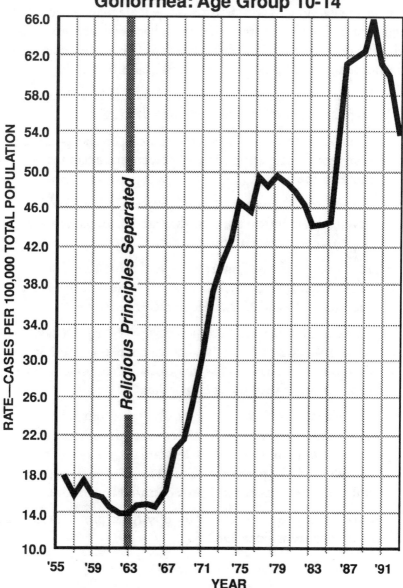

Basic data from the Center for Disease Control and
Department of Health and Human Resources.

Information on Student Sexual Activity

The previous graphs and statistics on teen pregnancies, teen births, and teen STDs clearly prove that there has been a dramatic explosion in adolescent sexual activity. How great has been that increase since students were denied access to Biblical principles?

- Premarital sexual activity among 15 year-old students has increased almost 1000 percent since 1962. [35]

- Over 40 percent of sexually active teens report having more than one sexual partner, and 20 percent have had four or more partners. [36]

- Two-thirds of America's 11 million teenage boys say they have had sex; and by the time they are 18, on the average, boys have had sex with five girls. [37]

- According to the Sex Information and Education Council of the U. S. (SIECUS), one of every three girls between the ages of 15 and 17 has had sexual intercourse. [38]

- Currently, 8,441 teens become sexually active each day; [39] most girls had their first sexual experience at age 15; [40] and half of sexually active males had their first sexual experience between the ages of 11 and 13. [41]

- Of those students who have gone through a comprehensive sex education program (a course promoting the "promiscuous intercourse of the sexes"), 65 percent are sexually active, a percentage almost twice as high as those who have not completed a sex-education curriculum. [42]

The following graphs document the upsurge in promiscuous sexual activity among teens since 1962-63:

Pre-Marital Sex

Percentage of U.S. Teenage Girls
Who Have Had Pre-Marital Intercourse

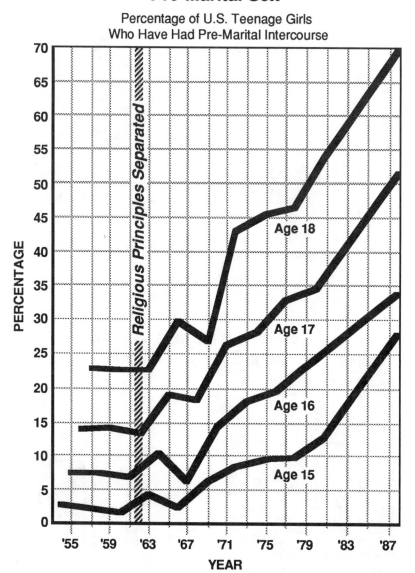

Basic data from *Family Planning Perspectives,* March/April 1987, and
from *Sexual and Reproductive Behavior of American Women, 1982-88.*
Furnished by the Alan Guttmacher Institute.

Teens Who Are Sexually Active

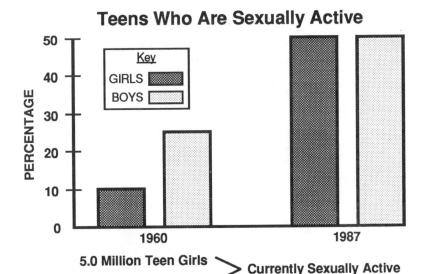

5.0 Million Teen Girls ⟩ Currently Sexually Active
6.5 Million Teen Boys

"Teenagers and Sex," *Parents*, January 1987, p.127.
"Young and Pregnant," *Parents*, March 1987, p. 196.

Male and Female Virgins
on a College Campus

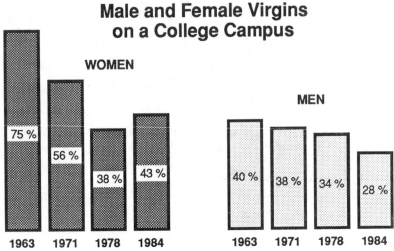

"New Sexual Attitudes," *Glamour*, Sept. 1985, p. 338. Taken from *Study of Sexual Behavior Spanning 21 Years.*
Robert Sherwin and Sherry Corbett, Miami University, Ohio.

Considering the sexual changes so evident in the lives of students, it is ironic that the Court forbids them access to Biblical teachings which promote self-control and internal restraints. It was signer and penman of the Constitution, Governeur Morris, who had explained:

> Religion is the only solid basis of good morals; therefore education should teach the precepts of religion, and the duties of man towards God. [43]

(A New Class of Problems)

Dramatic changes in student morality were not the only changes in student life following the Court decisions. Once the religious teachings which had long provided the basis for societal rights and wrongs were disallowed, students were encouraged to "discover" and to set their own standards: the consequences are now evident. Before the ban on religious teachings, the top public school problems were listed as: [44]

1. Talking
2. Chewing gum
3. Making noise
4. Running in the halls
5. Getting out of turn in line
6. Wearing improper clothing
7. Not putting paper in wastebaskets

Polls now list the top offenses as: [45]

1. Rape
2. Robbery
3. Assault
4. Burglary
5. Arson
6. Bombings
7. Murder
8. Suicide
9. Absenteeism
10. Vandalism
11. Extortion
12. Drug abuse
13. Alcohol abuse
14. Gang warfare
15. Pregnancies
16. Abortions
17. Venereal disease

So significant were the changes in student behavior following the Court decisions, that by 1965 the U. S. Department of Justice began to track youth violence as a separate category—something not previously done. The changes are astonishing:

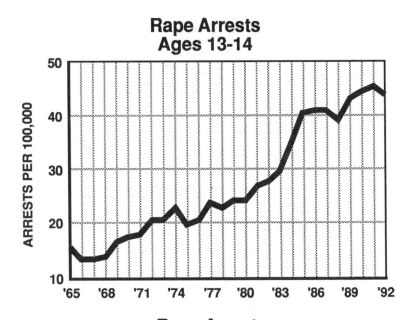

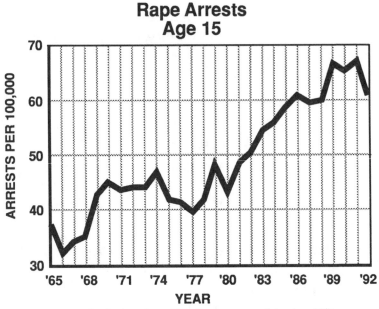

Basic data from U.S. Department of Justice, FBI.

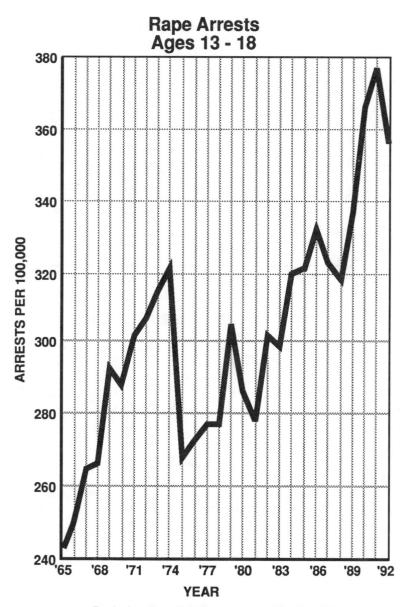

Rape Arrests
Ages 13 - 18

Basic data from U.S. Department of Justice, FBI.

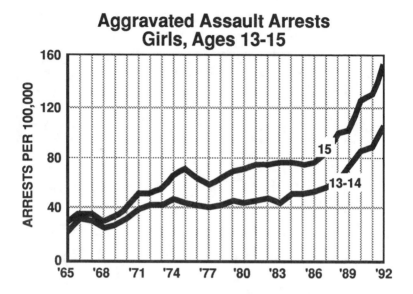

Aggravated Assault Arrests
Girls, Ages 13-15

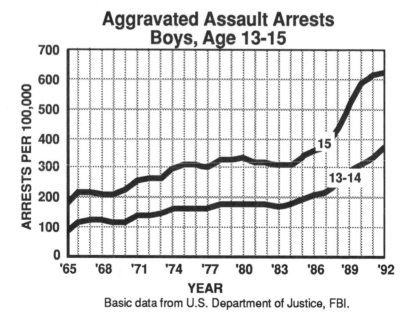

Aggravated Assault Arrests
Boys, Age 13-15

YEAR
Basic data from U.S. Department of Justice, FBI.

Aggravated Assault Arrests
Ages 13-18

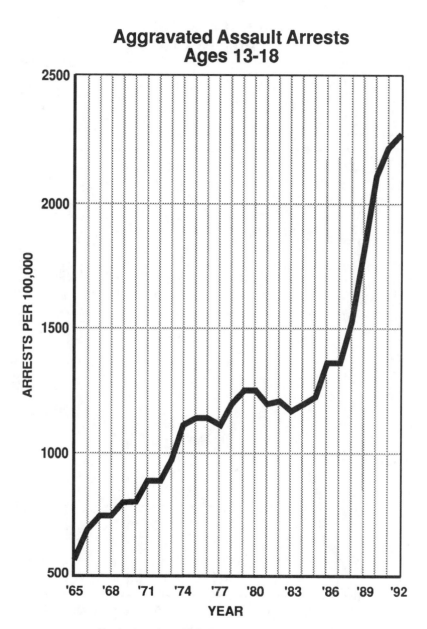

Basic data from U.S. Department of Justice, FBI.

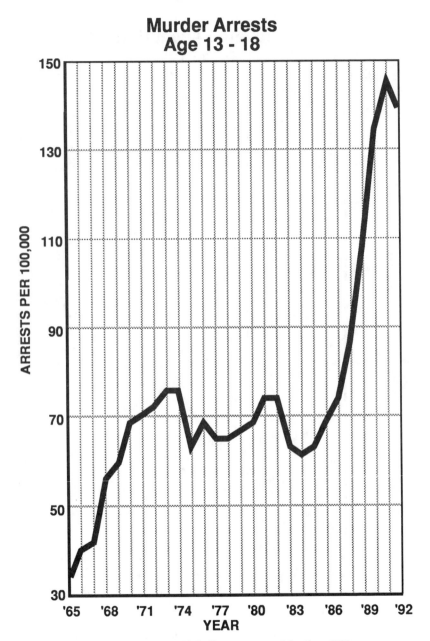

Murder Arrests
Age 13 - 18

Basic data from U.S. Department of Justice, FBI

The effect of this new moral-free approach to education is that the classroom no longer provides any restraining force on human passions—long seen as one of the primary purposes of public education. For example, in his 1794 address to the Massachusetts legislature, Governor Samuel Adams explained that:

> It has been observed that "education has a greater influence on manners than human laws can have." . . . [A] virtuous education is calculated to reach and influence the heart and to prevent crimes. . . . Such an education, which leads the youth beyond mere outside show, will impress their minds with a profound reverence of the Deity [and]. . . . will excite in them a just regard to Divine revelation. [46]

Founding Father Noah Webster, one of America's leading public educators, similarly declared:

> In my view, the Christian religion is the most important and one of the first things in which all children, under a free government, ought to be instructed. . . . No truth is more evident to my mind than that the Christian religion must be the basis of any government intended to secure the rights and privileges of a free people. The opinion that human reason, left without the constant control of divine laws and commands, will preserve a just administration, secure freedom and other rights, restrain men from violations of laws and constitutions, and give duration to a popular government, is as chimerical [unlikely] as the most extravagant ideas that enter the head of a maniac. . . . Where will you find any code of laws among civilized men in which the commands and prohibitions are not founded on Christian principles? I need not specify the prohibition of murder, robbery, theft [and] trespass. [47]

Benjamin Rush, a signer of the Declaration and the first Founding Father to call for free public schools, emphasized the same principle:

> The only foundation for a useful education in a republic is to be laid in religion. Without this, there can be no virtue, and without virtue there can be no liberty. [48] [T]he only means of establishing and perpetuating our republican forms of government . . . is the universal education of our youth in the principles of Christianity by means of the Bible; for this divine book above all others favors . . . respect for just laws. [49] Without religion, I believe that learning does real mischief to the morals and principles of mankind. [50]

Daniel Webster, a great American statesman reared at the feet of men like James Madison and Thomas Jefferson, explained:

> We regard it [public instruction] as a wise and liberal system of police by which property and life and the peace of society are secured. We seek to prevent in some measure the extension of the penal code by inspiring a salutary and conservative principle of virtue and of knowledge. [51] [However t]he attainment of knowledge does not comprise all which is contained in the larger term of education. The feelings are to be disciplined; the passions are to be restrained; true and worthy motives are to be inspired; a profound religious feeling is to be instilled, and pure morality inculcated. [52] The cultivation of the religious sentiment represses licentiousness . . . inspires respect for law and order, and gives strength to the whole social fabric. [53]

Religious principles had always been included in education because we understood the simple truth that crime could only be prevented by restraining the heart, and only religious principles were capable of accomplishing this feat. As John Quincy Adams noted:

Human legislators can undertake only to prescribe the actions of men; they acknowledge their inability to govern and direct the sentiments of the heart. . . . It is one of the greatest marks of Divine favor . . . that [God] gave . . . rules not only of action, but for the government of the heart. [54]

Since this powerful anti-crime influence has been separated from education, we probably should not be surprised at the results we now see; nevertheless, we are. Astonishingly, the most dramatic increases in violence are not seen among boys, but among girls. Since 1965:

- Assaults by girls ages 13-14 have increased by 377 percent; by 424 percent among 15 year-old girls; by 535 percent among 16 year-old girls; by 679 percent among 17 year-old girls; and by 577 percent among 18 year-old girls. [55]

- Murders by girls ages 13-14 have increased by 350 percent; by 450 percent among 15 year-old girls; and by 275 percent among 16 year-old girls. [56]

- Overall violent crimes have increased by 350 percent among 13-14 year-old girls; by 449 percent among 15 year-old girls; by 520 percent among 16 year-old girls; and by 572 percent among 17 year-old girls. [57]

While these increases in crimes committed by young girls is appalling, there have also been huge increases in crimes by young boys. For example, rapes by 13-14 year-old boys have increased 186 percent. [58] Additional information on the deteriorating attitudes of youth—both boys and girls—toward the issue of rape is provided by the Rhode Island Rape Crisis Center. In a survey of 1,700 sixth-through ninth-grade students (ages 12-15) in eight cities, [59] students were asked: "Under which situations does a man have a right to intercourse *against a woman's consent?*" As shown on the next page, their responses were both revealing and shocking:

Students' Attitudes Toward Rape		
Category	Percentages*	
It is okay for a man to force a woman to have sex against her consent if...	Boys	Girls
...he has been dating her for 6 to 12 months	65%	47%
...he spends as much as $10 to $15 on her	24%	16%
...they are planning to get married	74%	67%
...she had done it with other men	31%	32%

* The numbers in each column indicate the percentage of students who agreed with the statement.

Though the conditions varied, nearly one-half the students felt that there *were* situations which justified rape. With so many situations where rape is "acceptable," and with so many attitudes condoning it, the guarantee of a "safe" date no longer exists. The coordinator for the center conducting the research declared:

> So many of our kids have attitudes that sexual abuse is okay. I would . . . not have thought that 12- and 13-year-olds would think it's okay for a guy to force them to have intercourse with them. Such attitudes are probably triggering date rape and other forms of sexual assault. National statistics state that at least 25 percent of the girls in this country will be sexually assaulted before they turn 18. [60]

Nearly two-thirds of those who are sexually assaulted report that the assault was either date or acquaintance rape. [61] The fact that almost two-thirds of the attacks came from "friends" shows that self-indulgence has become the attitude of the day—gratify yourself no matter what the consequence to others.

The atrocious attitudes displayed in this study proceed directly from despising and/or ignoring the fundamental religious principles which were openly taught in public schools prior to 1962. [62] Perhaps a statement given by Robert Winthrop, a Speaker of the U. S. House of Representatives and a contemporary both of John Quincy Adams and of Daniel Webster, best explains the principle which today too many have forgotten; Winthrop wisely observed:

> Men, in a word, must necessarily be controlled, either by a power within them, or a power without them; either by the word of God, or by the strong arm of man; either by the Bible, or by the bayonet. [63]

Since the courts rule that we may no longer use "the Bible" in so many important public arenas, we have indeed resorted to "the bayonet," that is, to physical coercive force. Our legislatures now introduce an amazing 170,000 laws *per year,* most of which are attempting to restrain or prosecute criminal behavior. Since we no longer teach internal restraints, we must pursue external restraints. What signer Benjamin Rush predicted in 1791 has become true: by removing the Bible from schools, we now "waste so much time and money in punishing crimes, and take so little pains to prevent them." [64]

Chapter 4
"Our Parents"—The Family

Although the lives of students have changed dramatically since the removal of religious principles, the changes in families have been no less dramatic. A review of court decisions prior to 1962 will confirm that the court's family policies were based on traditional Biblical standards. Notice these representative rulings:

> Marriage was not originated by human law. When God created Eve, she was a wife to Adam; they then and there occupied the status of husband to wife and wife to husband. . . . When Noah was selected for salvation from the flood, he and his wife and his three sons and their wives were placed in the Ark; and, when the flood waters had subsided and the families came forth, it was Noah and his wife and each son and his wife. . . . The truth is that civil government has grown out of marriage . . . which created homes, and population, and society, from which government became necessary. . . . [Marriages] will produce a home and family that will contribute to good society, to free and just government, and to the support of Christianity. . . . It would be sacrilegious to apply the designation "a civil contract" to such a marriage. It is that and more; a status ordained by God. GRIGSBY v. REIB [1]

> This engagement [the legal contract of marriage] is the most solemn and important of human transactions. It is regarded by all Christian nations as the basis of civilized society, of sound morals, and of the domestic affections. . . . The mutual comfort and happiness of the parties are the principal, but not the only, objects of the engagement. It is intended also for the benefit of their common offspring and is an important element in the moral order, security and tranquility of civilized society. The parties cannot

dissolve the contract, as they can others, by mutual consent, and no light or trivial causes should be suffered to effect its recision. . . . [A]ccording to the experience of the most enlightened nations, the happiness of married life greatly depends on its indissolubility. SHEFFIELD v. SHEFFIELD [2]

The courts articulated this position which had first been declared by the Founding Fathers. For example, notice these remarks by Alexander Hamilton lamenting the evils of the French Revolution:

Equal pains have been taken to deprave the morals as to extinguish the religion of the country, if indeed morality in a community can be separated from religion. It is among the singular and fantastic vagaries [freaks] of the French Revolution that . . . a new law of divorce was passed which makes it as easy for a husband to get rid of his wife and a wife of her husband as to discard a worn out habit. . . . [T]hose ties . . . are the chief links of domestic and ultimately of social attachment. [3]

Other Founders spoke out on the importance of marriage:

The married state is, after all our jokes, the happiest, being conformable to our natures. Man and woman have each of them qualities and tempers in which the other is deficient and which in union contribute to the common felicity [happiness]. Single and separate, they are not the complete human being; they are like the odd halves of scissors; they cannot answer the end of their formation. [4] BENJAMIN FRANKLIN

In my estimation, more permanent and genuine happiness is to be found in the sequestered walks of connubial [married] life than in the giddy rounds of promiscuous pleasure or the more tumultuous and imposing scenes of successful ambition. [5] GEORGE WASHINGTON

James Wilson, a signer of the Constitution and a Justice of the U. S. Supreme Court, emphasized the importance of marriage and family in his legal commentaries on the Constitution. He explained:

> Whether we consult the soundest deductions of reason,
> or resort to the best information conveyed to us by history,
> or listen to the undoubted intelligence communicated in
> Holy Writ, we shall find that to the institution of marriage
> the true origin of society must be traced. By that institution
> the felicity of Paradise was consummated. . . . Legislators
> have with great propriety [correctness] . . . provided as far
> as municipal law can provide against the violation of rights
> indispensably essential to the purity and harmony of the
> matrimonial union. . . . By an act of the legislature . . . all
> marriages not forbidden by the law of God shall be
> encouraged. . . . But of causes which are light or trivial, a
> divorce should by no means be permitted to be the effect.
> When divorces can be summoned . . . a state of marriage
> becomes frequently a state of war. [6]

Similarly, founding judge James Kent, in his legal commentaries
on the Constitution, declared that:

> All Christian states favor the perpetuity of marriage, and
> suspicion and alarm watch every step to dissolve it. . . . Unlike
> other contracts, marriage cannot be dissolved by mutual
> consent. . . . The laws of divorce are considered as of the
> utmost importance as public laws affecting the dearest
> interests of society. . . . The domestic relation . . . of parent
> and child. . . . [and] the duties that reciprocally result from
> this connection are prescribed . . . by the positive precepts of
> religion and of our municipal law. [7]

Zephaniah Swift, a founding judge and author of America's first
law book, explained:

> The connection between husband and wife constitutes the
> most important and endearing relation that subsists
> between individuals of the human race. This union . . . is

productive of the purest joys and tenderest transports that gladden the heart. This connection between the sexes has been maintained in all ages, and in all countries. . . . All crimes that can be committed by an unchaste and illegal intercourse between the sexes are punished by the courts of common law. . . . It [divorce] destroys all that restraint upon the conduct of married persons which is imposed by the consideration that they cannot dissolve the connection. . . . The wisdom and good policy of this law [making divorces difficult] is evidenced by the consideration that in no country is a greater share of domestic felicity [happiness] enjoyed than in this state. [8]

Early courts echoed what the Founders intended, as evidenced by this decision in *Commonwealth* v. *Nesbit:*

[The Founders] did not mean that the pure moral customs which Christianity has introduced should be without legal protection because some pagan, or other religionist, or anti-religionist, should advocate as a matter of conscience concubinage, polygamy, incest, free love, and free divorce, or any of them. . . . No Christian people could possibly allow such things. [9]

Clearly, the heart of governmental policy, including that toward the family, had long been based on Biblical standards; if measured by the standards set forth in Washington's "Farewell Address," that long-standing policy had been a good one. He urged:

Observe good faith and justice toward all . . . cultivate peace and harmony with all. Religion and morality enjoin [encourage] this conduct. And can it be that good policy does not equally enjoin it? Can it be that Providence has not connected the permanent felicity [happiness] of a nation with its virtue? [10]

In Washington's opinion, religion and morality formed the basis for good policy. Nonetheless, in 1962-63, the Court adamantly rejected Washington's view of "good policy," adopting ill-advised policies like "no-fault divorce," thus making the changing of mates and the overturning of family stability as easy as the changing of a car or a residence. What have been the consequences? The results are evident on the following charts:

Divorce Rates

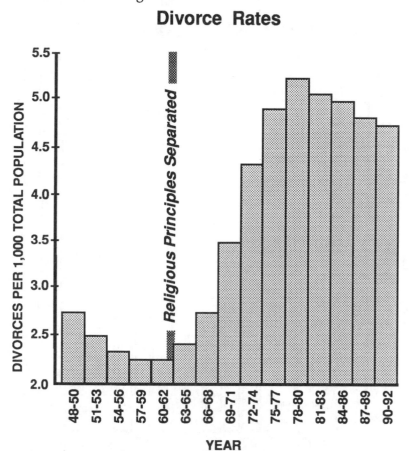

"The U.S. is at the top of the world's divorce charts on marital breakups."
U.S. News and World Report, June 8, 1987, pp. 68-69.

Basic data from the U. S. National Center for Health Statistics,
Vital Statistics of the United States, annual.

Even though the divorce rates seemed to show improvements after the late 70s, that decrease is deceptive. Simultaneous with that decrease was an explosion in the number of unmarried couples living together (see the following chart). Consequently, much of the reason for the divorce rates decreasing is that many couples now choose to live together rather than to get married; therefore, when they move on to a new partner, they no longer appear as a statistical divorce.

Unmarried Couples Living Together

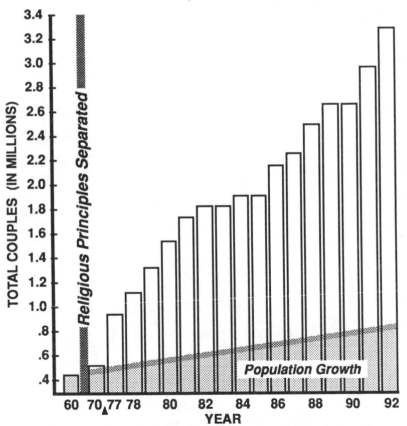

▲ Prior to 1977, unmarried couples living together was such a small group that data on this group was collected only in the 10-year census reports.

Basic data from *Statistical Abstracts of the United States.*

A further indication that the effects of divorce are not decreasing, regardless of the statistics, is seen in the measurements of single parent households; these numbers are still escalating:

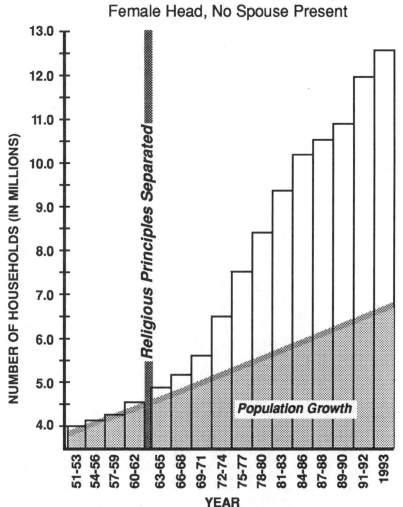

Single Parent Households
Female Head, No Spouse Present

Indicates population growth profile.

Basic data from *Statistical Abstracts of the United States,* and the Department of Commerce, Census Bureau.

In addition to the deterioration of family morality evidenced by unmarried couples living together, further evidence of decay is reflected by the upturn in adultery. Recall that the Founders predicted that the implementation of a policy of "free divorce" would be accompanied by an increase of "unchaste and illegal intercourse between the sexes." [11] Notice the accuracy of that prediction:

Adultery: Percentage
Involved in Extra-Marital Sex

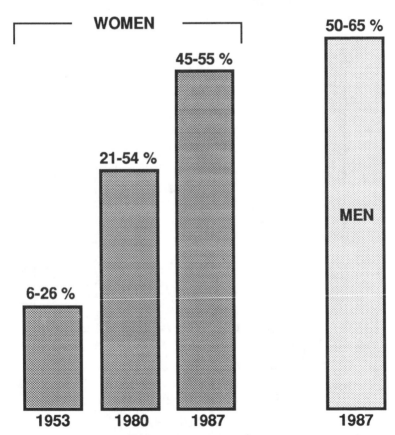

Basic data from "Unfaithfully Yours," *People*, August 18, 1986, p. 85, research by Alfred Kinsey; and "The News About Infidelity," *Cosmopolitan*, Apr. '87, p. 212, research by G.D. Nass, R.W. Libby, and M.P. Fisher.

Secondary Effects

The overall numbers reflecting the deterioration of the family are appalling: divorce rates are up almost 120 percent; the number of single parent families has increased 140 percent; unmarried couples living together have increased almost 600 percent; and adultery has skyrocketed.

Despite the openly permissive atmosphere which seems to wink at unmarried couples living together—and often encourages this as an alternative supposedly to avoid the trauma of divorce [12]—studies now prove that the negative impact from unmarried couples living together is even greater than that from divorce. For example:

- Physical aggression is more common among cohabiting couples than among married couples. [13]

- Those who cohabit are more likely to have drug, alcohol, personality problems, an inability to handle money, and a history of unemployment and trouble with the law. [14]

- Children seem to fare worse when their mothers live with a new partner without marriage. [15]

- Cohabiting women are 80 percent more likely to separate or divorce than women who did not live with their spouse before marriage. [16]

Another corollary effect of family breakups, both from unmarried couples living together and from divorce, is the problem of child abuse and runaways: [17]

- From 1.3 to 1.5 million children and youths run away from home each year. [18]

- Forty-three percent cite physical abuse as an important reason for leaving home. [19]

- Seventy-three percent of runaway girls and 38 percent of runaway boys report having been sexually abused. [20]

- Nearly half of runaways are between the ages of 15 and 16;[21] fifty-eight percent are female;[22] and forty-six percent are "pushouts" (youths whose parents push them out).[23]

- More than half of runaways come from households where one or both parents are alcoholics,[24] and nearly one-third come from single-parent homes.[25]

Additionally, runaways who are sexually abused are more likely to report suicidal feelings, to have trouble in school, to engage in delinquent and criminal activity, to participate in acts of violence, and to use alcohol and drugs.[26]

Summary

The devastation of the family following the Court's separation of religious principles from public policy makes Washington's warning worthy of review:

> Observe good faith and justice towards all . . . cultivate peace and harmony with all; religion and morality enjoin [encourage] this conduct and can it be that good policy does not equally enjoin it?[27]

Can it really be a good public policy to separate religious and moral principles from our public life? Statistical indicators strongly demonstrate otherwise.

Chapter 5
"Our Teachers"—American Education

With the eradication of most religious principles from education, a value-free environment has been created. The removal of moral absolutes and fixed rights and wrongs—including those so simple as the Ten Commandments—has unquestionably altered student morality and behavior, and as a direct result, student achievement.

Although many categories of educational statistics have measurements spanning decades, other categories are of recent origin and provide little basis for comparison of the present to the past. This is because statistics are rarely kept in what are considered non-problem areas. For example, measurements of illiteracy, school violence, and teacher competency were not kept two decades ago; the widespread nature of these problems is of recent origin. This chapter will examine the educational performance of America's schools and students in the period since the Court struck down the beliefs and practices which had long formed the foundation of American education.

The SAT Test

The Scholastic Aptitude Test (SAT) is a test which measures verbal and math skills of prospective college-bound students. First administered to high-school students in 1926, a common scale was established in 1941 to allow annual comparisons of the scores, thus enabling "apples with apples" comparisons to be made over the past half-century. As evidenced on the following charts, student achievement has declined dramatically since 1962.

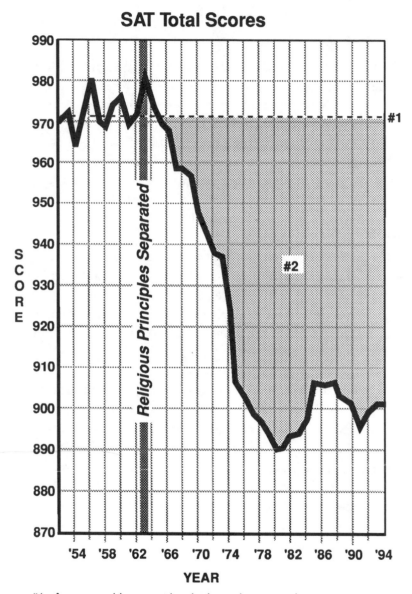

SAT Total Scores

#1 - Average achievement level prior to the separation

#2 - Amount of reduced academic achievement since the separation

Basic data from the College Entrance Exam Board.

SAT Verbal Scores

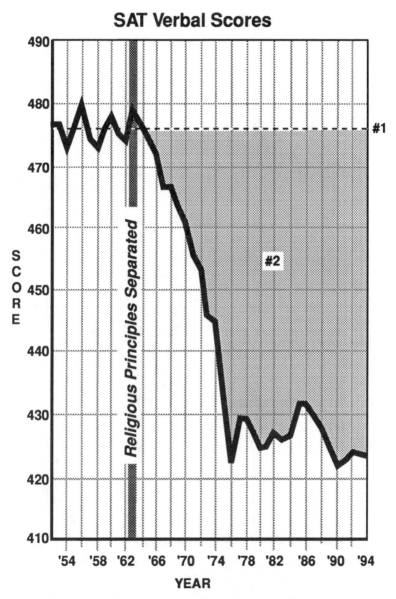

#1 - Average achievement level prior to the separation
#2 - Amount of reduced academic achievement since the separation

Basic data from the College Entrance Exam Board.

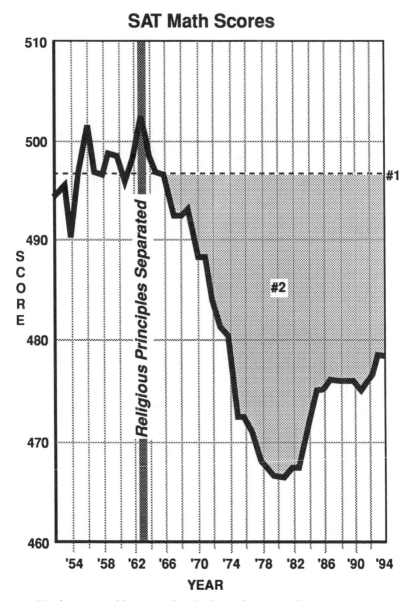

SAT Math Scores

#1 - Average achievement level prior to the separation

#2 - Amount of reduced academic achievement since the separation

Basic data from the College Entrance Exam Board.

Prior to 1962-63, SAT scores had never declined more than two years in a row; however, the Court decisions were followed by eighteen *consecutive* years of decline—unprecedented in the history of the SAT. Interestingly, the rate of decline began slowing in the mid-70s, and in 1981 scores actually began improving until 1987 when they again turned downward (note the graph below):

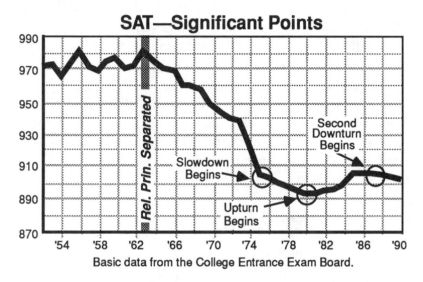

SAT—Significant Points

Basic data from the College Entrance Exam Board.

If the removal of religious principles did result in the original downturn in 1962-63, then what would explain the slowdown in the 70s and subsequent upturn begun in 1981? After all, religious principles had not been reinstated in education.

Significantly, during those years, a national educational movement emerged which correlates with each point of change on the chart: the growth in private school enrollment. For example, occurring simultaneously with the slowdown of declining scores in the 70s was a corresponding explosion in the number of students entering private schools. According to Department of Education figures, between 1974-1984, private school enrollment jumped 17 percent, reaching some 8,465,000 students by 1984. That strong private school growth is particularly impressive because population figures show that the total number of students attending all schools in the nation was actually decreasing during the same time. Further, the majority of the growth in the private school movement occurred among religious schools (85 percent of private-school students attend religiously-affiliated schools [1]).

As an example of the astounding growth in the Christian school movement, in 1974, Accelerated Christian Education (ACE) had 479 affiliate schools; by 1984, that number had jumped to over 6,000 schools with more than 240,000 students. At the Association of Christian Schools International (ACSI), the number of students in affiliated schools increased from 186,000 in 1978, to 475,000 in 1989. The American Association of Christian Schools (AACS) represented only 125 schools with 16,000 students in 1972; but by 1990, that number had climbed to 1,200 schools with 165,000 students. The *Washington Post* [2] presented a table depicting the Christian school explosion:

CHRISTIAN SCHOOLS IN THE UNITED STATES

YEAR	SCHOOLS
1965	1,000
1970-71	2,500
1980-81	7,500
1984-85	*13,000

PROJECTED

Even though 13,000 Christian schools were projected for the end of the 1984-85 school year, that projection turned out to be quite low. Paul A. Kienel, president of ACSI, reports that a curriculum publisher conducted a search in the Library of Congress and could account for more than 32,000 Christian schools! This growth trend among religious/private school enrollment which began in the mid-70s continued until 1987 when enrollment in those schools began to decline.

Notice the correlation: as the number of students in religious/private schools was growing, the scores were gradually recovering and even improving from their dramatic slide; however, when the number of students attending those schools began to fall, scores once again turned downward. While this correlation is of interest, the only plausible way that students from religious/private schools could have impacted the SAT scores positively would be if they were achieving higher scores than their counterparts in public schools. Was this the case?

In 1987, the College Board began to isolate SAT scores in a manner which allowed for comparisons of scores between students from religious/private schools and their peers in public schools. The results are shown on the following graph:

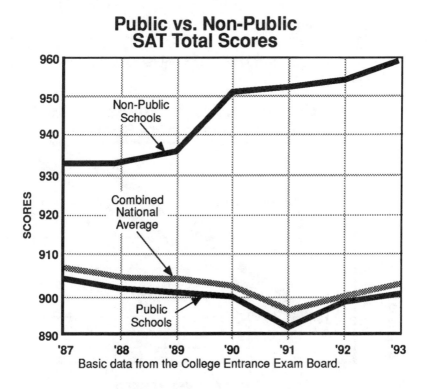

Public school scores are not only lower than private school scores, they are also lower than the national totals, demonstrating that were it not for the positive effect of the religious/private scores, the SAT scores would be even *lower* than they currently are. The disparity between public and non-public scores since 1987 is great enough to suggest that the same differences probably existed prior to 1987. Furthermore, the fact that the total national scores began to decline in 1987 despite the still improving religious/private scores simply indicates that there were not enough private school students to pull the national totals upward against the greater pressure of the increased numbers of public school students pulling the scores downward.

The SAT is not the only test showing higher religious/private scores; another is the Stanford Achievement Test, used nationally throughout both public and private schools. ACSI uses this test in their 2,700 affiliate Christian schools with their 475,000 students; notice the difference between Christian school and public school achievement on the identical test:

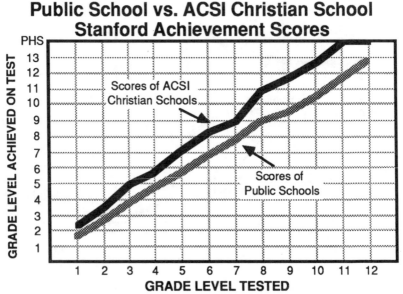

Basic data from The Psychological Corporation, 1988 testing results.

Still another academic test revealing similar disparities is the PSAT-NMSQT (Preliminary Scholastic Aptitude Test—National Merit

Scholarship Qualifying Test). Of those taking the test, the top 1/2 percentile from each state—considered that state's academic "cream of the crop"— qualify as semifinalists from National Merit Scholarships. In the 1988 testing, of the 1,213,042 students participating, only 15,414 qualified as semifinalists. A survey was undertaken to determine which percentages of these academic elite students were produced by religious/ private schools and which by public schools.

According to the Department of Education, at the time of the testing, 12.4 percent of students attended religious/private schools. Therefore, 12.4 percent of the semifinalists should have been produced by those schools. Such was not the case; surprisingly, the survey revealed that 39.2 percent of the top academic achievers— and not the expected 12.4 percent—came from religious/private schools. (The detailed results of that survey are provided in Appendix C.) The following graph illustrates the disproportionately positive impact of private schools on testing results:

Student Population vs. Achievement

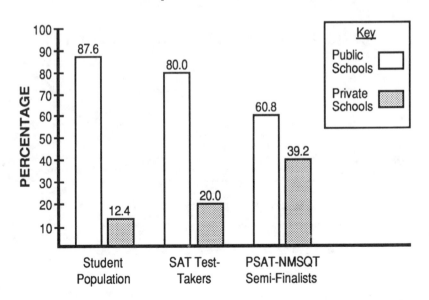

The fact that religious/private schools proportionally . . .

. . . produce 1.6 times more SAT-takers than their relative population (20 percent as opposed to 12.4 percent);

. . . produce 3.2 times more academically elite students than their relative population (39.2 percent as opposed to 12.4 percent);

. . . produce students at all grade levels with higher achievement scores than their public school counterparts,

strongly demonstrates that religious/private schools are having a positive academic effect dramatically greater than their proportional strength.

Some have tried to dismiss this stark difference in performance by asserting that affluence is the major reason private schools surpass public schools in academic achievements. However, when the money expended per student in private schools (an indicator of affluence) is compared with public schools, it is apparent that money is less than a significant factor in private school achievement:

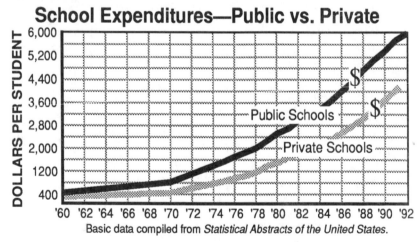

School Expenditures—Public vs. Private

Basic data compiled from *Statistical Abstracts of the United States.*

Private schools, spending much less money per student, attain higher achievement. Furthermore, private school families are penalized for their higher achievement in that they must pay for their children's education twice: not only do they pay public school taxes, they also must pay private school tuitions/fees. Therefore, when the average tuition cost of only *one* student (and the statistically "typical" family contains two children) is deducted from the income of private-school families, those families often have *less* unrestricted money available for their children than do public school families, further disparaging the notion that affluence produces achievement.

An observation should be made here: there is no fundamental difference in the core curriculum between religious/private schools and public schools. The Civil War occurs the same years at both schools; math tables remain the same; and a verb does not become an adjective merely because a student attends a religious school. Therefore, since the core academic curriculum—the basis for educational testing—is fundamentally the same for both types of schools, the measurable differences in academic achievement must stem from the educational philosophy under which the curriculum is applied. At least 85 percent of that group of schools achieving higher performance includes religious principles and moral standards as an inherent part of their educational philosophy and instructional process.

Conflicting Academic Standards

An interesting enigma has now materialized in educational testing: during the same period that student achievement scores have dramatically fallen, their report card scores have actually risen—an oxymoron depicted on the following two graphs.

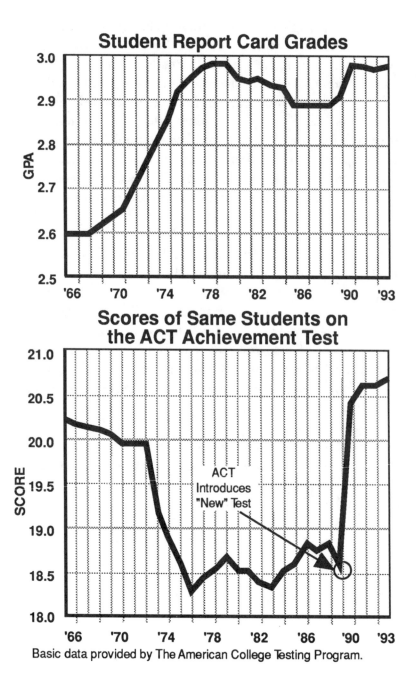

Student Report Card Grades

Basic data provided by The American College Testing Program.

Amazingly, students have been receiving higher marks in school while their achievement has been decreasing! Note the point on the chart where a "new" test was introduced. The "new" test means that it was "renormed"; that is, a new reference "standard" for measuring the students' knowledge was introduced. Observe how much the student scores improved immediately after the renorming; students are now apparently smarter than any previous students in the history of the test—and that dramatic improvement occurred over the span of only *one* year! Renorming simply takes what once was the lower level and raises it to become the average level with scores making the same shift; renorming is simply a subjective, rather than an objective, recategorization of what will constitute "average." Renorming of tests gives new meaning to the phrase "upward mobility."

International Testing

While our students seem to perform well when measured by our renormed domestic standards, their true academic weaknesses become apparent when they are tested against their peers in other nations. Although the U. S. has participated in international academic competition for decades, we have never had the results we now do. In recent years:

- International comparisons of student achievement reveal that on 19 academic tests, American students were *never* first or second and, in comparison with other industrialized nations, were *last* seven times. [3]

- In a test comparing average American public school sixth-graders with their counterparts in seven other Western industrialized countries, American public school students ranked *last* in mathematics and not much better in science and geography. [4]

- Our 14-year-old science students placed 14th out of 17 competing countries. Advanced American science students were 9th of 13 countries in physics, 11th of 13 in chemistry, and *last* in biology. [5]

- In a testing of 12th grade students among 11 nations, the United States placed *last* in algebra and was ahead of only Hungary in calculus. When considering only the brightest students—the top five percent of each category—the United States was *last* in both algebra and calculus. [6]

- In an international assessment of math and science among six developed countries, American students ranked *last* in mathematics and next to last overall in science. [7]

The poor performance of American students on international math competitions in recent decades, particularly after our excellent performance in previous decades, prompted further investigation into the math abilities of American students. Notice some of the findings:

- A University of Michigan study of math achievement among fifth-graders found that the highest-achieving American class did worse than the lowest-performing Japanese class. [8]

- A University of Illinois at Chicago study found that the average American high school student would rank 99th in math when compared with 100 average Japanese students. [9]

(**Trans-National Studies**)

Perhaps the lack of respect that America's educational system now receives from the international community is best illustrated by the results of a two-year study conducted between Japan and the United States. Teams of scholars from each nation made extensive visits to the other's schools to search for ingredients which would be helpful for their own educational system.

At the conclusion of the study, the U. S. Department of Education released its findings in the report *Japanese Education Today,* accompanied by an epilogue entitled "Implications for American Education." These reports noted numerous aspects of the Japanese system which the researchers felt should be incorporated into the American system.* Japanese officials released their report at the same time and had reached a very definite conclusion: they found *nothing* they wanted to copy!

> "It is not our intention that contents of the current American educational system ... be proposed as elements of educational reform in Japan," the study said. "Recently, the outcome of common math tests show Japanese kids scoring higher than Americans," said Mr. Amagi, who led the study for the Ministry of Education. "American scholars," Mr. Amagi went on, "seem to share the view that the American educational system has fallen into mediocrity. American kids register very bad scores on international tests." Quoting from recent studies by American educators, the Japanese researchers cited the worries in the United States about teacher skills, dropout rates, poor student performance and lowered college standards. [10]

It is a potent commentary on the current state of American education that after two years of extensive study, the Japanese researchers could find "no specific aspect of American education ... considered worth emulating." [11]

(Teacher Competency Testing)

With the growing concern for poor student performance, attention has begun to focus not only on the educational system in general, but on teachers in particular. Consequently, several states began requiring teacher competency testing; notice these results from Texas:

---

* The conclusion of the American investigators is ironic: the current Japanese educational system is actually the American educational system of the late 1940s which was placed in Japan by the United States as part of reconstruction after World War II! Members of General Douglas MacArthur's staff who personally participated in building that system during the 1940s and 50s have commented that the successful elements of the Japanese system have changed little since the time of their implementation in the late 1940s. Therefore, the contrasts between Japan's current educational successes and our failures become even more painful when realizing that Japan's present system is actually built on the American educational system of a half-century ago.

- When the [competency] test was given to 1,269 college juniors in Texas teacher education programs, 38 percent failed the exam, which [only] tests basic skills taught by the 12th grade, such as calculating percentages, capitalizing words, and comprehending a 200-word passage. [12]

- The test was also given to 3,300 new teachers in the Houston Independent School District. Because of cheating and other irregularities, scores for only 2,400 of the teachers were reported. Almost two-thirds—62 percent—failed the exam. The Houston School Board later lowered the passing score so that only 44 percent of the teachers failed. [13]

- Dallas school officials say that on the same test, 54 percent of the 2,280 teachers hired by the Dallas school district since 1979 could not correctly answer 67 percent of the questions. [14]

With similar startling results occurring in a number of states, twenty-six states have now begun to test teachers. According to a report prepared by the Department of Education (*What's Happening in Teacher Testing*), 17 percent of those who had *already* received their college education degrees *failed* teacher certification testing! [15] Furthermore, since the average score required to pass the exam was only around 50 percent, it is a very generous statement to report that only 17 percent of the applicants are unqualified. Had the passing mark been raised to the barely minimum 70 percent, the percentage of "unqualified" teachers would have risen significantly.

Since the Bible teaches that "a student will become like his teacher" (Luke 6:40), it is appropriate to be concerned about teacher competency. According to statistics made available during a White House briefing attended by the author in September 1989, 700,000 students *graduated* from high-school in June 1986 unable to read their own diplomas!

The generally diminishing academic abilities of students has resulted in a 72 percent increase in the number of colleges and universities offering remedial courses to accommodate the lower skill levels of new college entrants. [16] Such a lowering produces weaker degree programs, which results in weaker college graduates, many of whom will re-enter the educational arena as weaker teachers. These weaker teachers will in turn produce even weaker students, that in turn will produce even weaker degree programs in colleges and universities, that in turn will produce even weaker teachers, that in turn. . . . To reproduce this scenario on a continuing basis is unacceptable, yet this is what is currently happening: since 1973, the SAT scores of prospective teachers have fallen 55 points, [17] and the Department of Education reports that "half of the *newly qualified* mathematics, science, and English teachers are not qualified to teach these subjects." [18]

School Violence

As documented in chapter 3, there have been dramatic increases in general society concerning violence by juveniles. However, their violence is now carried onto the school campus, and to suggest that violence in schools is now a problem is a mammoth understatement. News articles such as the following from the *Los Angeles Times* have become commonplace across the nation:

> At most of the Oakland Unified School District's 92 schools, the fight against crime and violence is unending. An Uzi semiautomatic rifle, with 15 hollow-point bullets, was among the weapons confiscated by district officials within the last year. Franklin Elementary School . . . trying to ensure that students know to hit the ground when bullets fly, carries out "shooting" drills twice a year. [19]

From the *Fort Worth Star-Telegram*:

> School officials learned about the most recent [sexual] assault Friday after investigators talked to the 11-year-old victim. The sixth-grade student . . . was assaulted on two occasions at school while she waited for her parents to pick her up. The girl told investigators that two 13-year-

old boys raped her in a girls' restroom at school two weeks ago. On Thursday, one of the same boys and three of his friends returned to where she again was waiting. The girl told police the boys took her back into the school against her will, and two of them raped her behind a stairwell while the other two watched, according to a police report. A 15-year-old girl told police she was assaulted May 10 in an empty ROTC room.... She named an 18-year-old student as her attacker. Another assault reportedly occurred May 11 behind a stage curtain in a . . . school auditorium. The 16-year-old victim told police she was held by two students while a third raped her. [20]

From the *New York Times* on Detroit's schools:

On the average, a child was shot every day in 1986.... The city canceled classes Monday and today to hold assemblies on youth violence. Just before spring break . . . a 14-year-old student firing a .357 magnum pistol chased a star football player through the halls of Murray-Wright High School . . . as others looked on helpless and in horror. The football player was killed by a bullet to the head. Two other students were wounded. Parents are demanding metal detectors and searches for weapons in the schools. The call for searches has reignited a debate that raged a few years ago, when officials conducted random searches for a time but stopped after the American Civil Liberties Union sued. . . . City officials said they would resume weapons searches in the schools. "I'm tired of kids carrying guns like they used to take a lunch," Mayor Coleman Young said. [21]

The *Chicago Sun-Times* reported:

A new security program that brought 150 police officers into the Chicago public schools resulted in an unprecedented 4,306 arrests [at school] in the first four months of this school year.... Police made nearly 14 times the number of drug arrests as had been made in the previous fall and nearly 12 times the weapons arrests.... There were 1,122 arrests for disorderly conduct ... 910 for battery and 738 for criminal trespass ... 229 [for] alleged weapons violations. ... "I'm proud of the fact we're taking action to reduce the level of violence in the schools" [said George H. Sams, head of security for Chicago's 600 public schools]. [22]

Even the trends in student fashions speak loudly:

Bulletproof back-to-school clothes are the latest thing for ... children who run a dangerous gauntlet to and from class. School blazers and other jackets [are] fitted with bullet-resistant Kevlar 129 pads....Added shielding from flying bullets can be had from a bulletproof book bag or clipboard. They're offered by [a] former New York City police officer. [23]

The "Safe Schools Study" by the National Institute of Education reported: [24]

- Only 17 to 19 percent of violent offenses against urban youths 12 to 15 occur in the street. Sixty-eight percent of the robberies and 50 percent of the assaults on youngsters of this age occur at school.
- 282,000 secondary school students reported that they were attacked at school in a typical one-month period.
- The risk of violence to teenagers is greater in public schools than elsewhere.

Boston's Safe Schools Commission found: [25]

- Nearly 4 out of 10 students were often fearful for their safety in school or reported avoiding certain locations like corridors and restrooms.

- 3 out of 10 students admitted carrying weapons to school.
- Half of the teachers and 40 percent of the students had been victims of school robbery, assault, or larceny.

Other statistics are equally distressing: [26]

- 5,200 high-school teachers are physically attacked each month, with one-fifth requiring medical treatment.
- Attacks on teachers are five times more likely to result in serious injury than attacks on students.
- Only one in three offenses committed on school campuses is reported to school officials.

Student Suicides

Not only have students become violent toward others, they have become violent toward themselves. Suicides among youth 15-24 have increased 253 percent since 1962-63. [27] Minimum estimates indicate that 400,000 adolescents attempt suicide each year; [28] other estimates place the attempts at nearly 2,000,000 per year—one every 15 seconds. In 1962, suicide ranked 12th in the cause of death among young people; in 1990, it ranked 3rd. [29]

Basic Subject Knowledge Lacking

Any environment where disrespect, immorality, and violence prevail is certainly not conducive to effective learning, as confirmed by the numerous graphs in this chapter. The startling lack of basic student academic knowledge in the most fundamental subjects is becoming more and more apparent. For example, following the results of a survey of five-thousand high-school seniors in eight major cities, members of the U. S. Senate moved to designate a "Geography Awareness Week." Why? [30]

- 25 percent of the seniors tested in Dallas could not identify the country that borders the United States on the south.

- 39 percent of the seniors in Boston could not name the six New England states.

- 45 percent of the seniors in Baltimore could not respond correctly to this instruction: "On the attached map, shade in the area where the United States is located."

Similar weaknesses were recorded in a survey conducted among college students: [31]

- When asked to identify the two largest states, fewer than half of them could name Texas and Alaska.

- Almost 80 percent couldn't name the two smallest states.

Geography is not the only subject where students exhibit substandard knowledge; the same problem afflicts basic U. S. History. Following an assessment of 17 year-old students (80 percent of whom were enrolled in U. S. History classes at the time of the testing), the Department of Education reported: "Many students are unaware of prominent people and seminal ideas and events that have shaped our past and created our present." [32] What prompted that conclusion?

- Almost half of the students could not place World War I between 1900 and 1950.

- More than two-thirds did not know when the Civil War took place.

- More than 75 percent were unable to say within 20 years when Abraham Lincoln was President.

- One-fifth of the students could not identify George Washington as the commander of the Colonial forces during the Revolution.

- One-third did not know that Lincoln was the author of the Emancipation Proclamation.

- One-half failed to recognize Patrick Henry as the man who said, "Give me liberty or give me death!"

- One-third did not know that the Declaration of Independence signaled the American Colonists' break from England.

- Almost half could not say even approximately when the Constitution was written.

Following the dismal performance of high-school seniors in American history, a similar assessment was then conducted of college seniors; the results were appalling: [33]

- One-fourth thought Christopher Columbus landed in the Western Hemisphere after 1500 (he landed in 1492).

- One-third thought the Magna Carta (signed 1215 A.D.) was what the Pilgrims signed on the Mayflower (1620 A.D.; the Pilgrims signed the Mayflower Compact).

- Two-fifths thought the Emancipation Proclamation was a document from the Constitutional Convention of 1787 (rather than the 1863 document by Abraham Lincoln).

- One-third thought that Jamestown, Virginia, was founded after 1750 (it was founded in 1606).

- One-fifth thought "The Shot Heard 'Round the World" was fired at Gettysburg (it was fired in Lexington in 1775, not Gettysburg in 1863).

After sixteen years of formal educational studies, many college seniors still have no basic working knowledge of American History.

(American Education and Business)

This unprecedented decline in basic student knowledge is threatening the business community; many American businesses have been forced to restructure their programs to accommodate weaker students. The reason for that restructuring is obvious:

- New York Telephone Company gave its simple 50-minute exam in basic reading and reasoning skills to 21,000 applicants for entry-level jobs. Only 16 percent passed. [34]

- A Department of Education study asked young adults with a college degree to answer this question: "If you spend $1.95 for a sandwich and 60 cents for a bowl of soup, and give the cashier $3, how much change should you receive?" The answer is 45 cents, but one-third of the college graduates missed it. [35]

- A number of banks in the New York City public school district agreed to place some 400 students into entry level positions. [36] The bank's criterion for employment was nothing more than simple, standard job entry skills, but they were able to qualify only 100 students. The others did not even have the basic reading and writing skills required for employment. [37]

Skills are so low among potential workers that many corporations are setting aside huge portions of their annual budget for remedial education for employees. For example, Xerox Executives report:

American business will have to hire more than a million new service and production workers a year who can't read, write or count. Teaching them how, and absorbing the lost productivity while they are learning, will cost industry $25 billion a year, and nobody seems to know how long such remedial training will be necessary. Three out of four major corporations already are giving new workers basic reading, writing and arithmetic courses . . . Corporate training is bigger than our entire elementary, secondary and higher education system put together. . . . It is a terrible admission, but $25 billion a year for remedial training has become a necessary added cost of doing business.

Another business executive gives a similar report:

> While working for Chrysler Corp., John C. Graves found . . . that the majority of new assembly line workers hired (most of them recent high-school graduates) could read at only a sixth-grade level and do only fourth-grade math. He blames the curriculum and promotion policies of schools: "These people should never have gotten out of school in the first place." Now training and development manager at a Rockwell International plant that makes nuclear devices in Colorado, Graves finds that nearly all new assembly line employees need basic skills training before they can learn their jobs. Employees must read and compute at a seventh- to ninth-grade level to be trainable at his plant, Graves said. "We're finding that a majority of people are not coming into the work place with skills that high." [38]

Motorola executives also lament our academic weaknesses:

> Motorola feels it must supplement the skills of entry-level workers who "have nowhere near the mathematical competence of our Japanese competitors," says Edward W. Bales, director of operations. . . . Mr. Bales cites a recent study by the federally-funded International Association for the Evaluation of Education Achievement, which found, among other things, that elementary-school pupils in Japan had reached the same level of math competence as junior-high-school students in the U. S. [39]

Ironically, in the face of these deficiencies, school officials still claim that students *are* prepared to enter the work force:

> A report published by the Center for Public Resources . . . [found that] while most companies reported basic skills deficiencies in most job categories, over 75 percent of the school system rated their graduates as "academically prepared" in the basic academic skills needed for employment. [40]

American Education and the Armed Forces

The same weaknesses which make so many high school graduates academically unfit for business also prevent them from meeting even the minimum requirements for the military. For example, the Navy is now forced to provide remedial training for its recruits:

> A . . . study of naval personnel, authorized last year by Admiral Watkins, recently retired Chief of Naval Operations . . . found that more than 20 percent of [recruits] . . . were unable to read at the ninth-grade level, the minimum level required for dealing with technical manuals that are essential to their training and job skills. He added that 97 percent of those who could not make it through boot camp—mainly because of their flawed knowledge of reading—had high school diplomas. . . . Of the 1.9 million young men who now enter the labor force each year . . . about 600,000 are unfit for military service without extensive remedial training. . . . "We know from experience that, of that 600,000, we can remediate at least half," he said. "Why aren't they remediated ahead of time?" [41]

The same problems exist in the Air Force and Army:

> Three years ago, 54 percent of the 18-year-olds in the United States were qualified to enter the Air Force; today that has dropped to 34 percent . . . Although 98 percent of the recruits now have high school diplomas, the Air Force still finds itself with people who can't read at the ninth-grade level, which is necessary to complete training. The number of Army recruits whose reading and math abilities are below the ninth-grade level increased sharply during the past decade. . . . [T]he Army has spent more than $160 million . . . to provide remedial education for recruits. [42]

An Overview of American Education

As one examines the current condition of American education, there is justification for concern. Even the Department of Education offers a bleak assessment of American education, noting: [43]

- For the first time in the history of our country, the educational skills of one generation will not surpass, will not equal, will not even approach, those of their parents.

- Thirty-five states require only 1 year of mathematics, and 36 require only 1 year of science for a high-school diploma.

- In 13 states, 50 percent or more of the units required for high school graduation may be electives chosen by the student. Given this freedom, many students opt for less demanding personal service courses, such as bachelor living.

- In many schools, the time spent learning how to cook and drive counts as much toward a high school diploma as the time spent studying mathematics, English, chemistry, American history, or biology.

- Nearly 40 percent of 17-year-olds cannot draw inferences from written material, and only a third can solve a math problem requiring several steps.

- A recent study revealed that a majority of students were able to master 80 percent of the material in some of their texts before they had even opened the books.

- A study of the typical public school schedule found that the average school provided only 22 hours of academic instruction during the week.

In recent decades there have been numerous attempts to reverse the academic deterioration by improving student/teacher ratio, by increasing teacher salaries, by elevating spending on public education, etc.; yet despite these efforts, the quality of education has continued to decline. (For more information on the statistical results of these efforts, see the author's booklet *What Happened In Education?)* Benjamin Franklin's rebuff to the delegates at the Constitutional Convention seems appropriate here:

> In this situation . . . how has it happened, Sir, that we have not hitherto once thought of humbly applying to the Father of lights . . . Have we now forgotten this powerful Friend? Or do we imagine we no longer need His assistance? . . . We have been assured, Sir, in the Sacred Writings that except the Lord build the house, they labor in vain that build it. I firmly believe this; and I also believe that without His concurring aid, we shall succeed . . . no better than the builders of Babel. [44]

The extensive energy expended on our public educational system over recent decades has all been without asking—to the contrary, forbidding—any assistance of God. Measurements confirm that, to a large part, those labors have been wasted (recall, however, that substantially higher academic achievements *are* recorded by schools which embrace God and His principles). Franklin's conclusion appears true: "Except the Lord build the house, they labor in vain that build it" (Psalms 127:1).

Chapter 6
"Our Country"—The Nation

As with each previous category, the courts had consistently ruled before 1962 with Biblical principles forming the basis of national policy, even declaring that Christianity was a part of the common law (i.e., the foundation on which all other laws rested). Notice these representative rulings:

> This wise legislature framed this great body of laws for a Christian country and Christian people. . . . This is the Christianity of the common law. . . . in this the Constitution of the United States has made no alteration. . . . No free government now exists in the world unless where Christianity is acknowledged and is the religion of the country . . . [I]t is the . . . only stable support of all human laws. UPDEGRAPH v. COMMONWEALTH [1]

> Christianity is part of the common law of the land. . . . It has always been so recognized. . . . The U. S. Constitution allows it as a part of the common law. . . . In the Courts over which we preside, we daily acknowledge Christianity as the most solemn part of our administration. A . . . witness . . . [places] his hand upon . . . the books of the New Testament which testify of our Savior's birth, life, death, and resurrection; this is so common a matter that it is little thought of as an evidence of the part which Christianity has in the common law. CHARLESTON v. S. A. BENJAMIN [2]

> Whatever strikes at the root of Christianity tends manifestly to the dissolution of civil government . . . because it tends to corrupt the morals of the people, and to destroy good order. PEOPLE v. RUGGLES [3]

Despite a lengthy history of numerous cases filled with similar declarations, contemporary courts first ignored, then reversed this policy. Many have now engaged in indiscriminate warfare against the very principles they once protected. For example, in the late-50s, there were almost no legal challenges against religious principles in public arenas; by the mid-70s, there were eighty-four; [4] and by the early-90s, the number of legal challenges had soared to over 3,000! [5] The message of the courts is clear: religious expressions are no longer welcome in public affairs. This current policy, judged by the warnings of the Founders, is a blueprint for domestic disaster. George Washington stated:

> Of all the dispositions and habits which lead to political prosperity, religion and morality are indispensable supports. In vain would that man claim the tribute of patriotism, who should labour to subvert [overturn] these great pillars. . . . Let it simply be asked, "Where is the security for property, for reputation, for life, if the sense of religious obligation desert . . . ?" [6]

Noah Webster, the Founder responsible for portions of Article I, Section 8 of the Constitution, similarly warned:

> The moral principles and precepts contained in the Scriptures ought to form the basis of all our civil constitutions and laws. . . . All the miseries and evils which men suffer from vice, crime, ambition, injustice, oppression, slavery, and war, proceed from their despising or neglecting the precepts contained in the Bible. [7]

Webster's warning, coupled with that of Washington, forms an incredibly accurate prediction of what has occurred in the nation: the loss of safety for property and life caused by increases in crime and vice since the Court began "despising or neglecting the precepts contained in the Bible."

The Cause and Effects of Crime

The Founders understood that government was unable to control crime apart from Christian principles. Thomas Jefferson once noted:

> The precepts of philosophy and of the Hebrew [legal] code laid hold of actions only. He [Jesus] pushed his scrutinies into the heart of man [and] erected his tribunal in the region of his thoughts. [8]

Jefferson understood the weakness of civil laws: they were unable to address the heart—the actual seat of violence, crime, immorality, and all other dereliction. Only religious principles can stop a crime before it occurs; only religion can deal with murder while it is still only a thought in the heart; civil and criminal laws can do nothing until after the fact. This principle was widely understood, and thus the Founders refused to allow the uncoupling of religious principles from government:

> The law given from Sinai was a civil and municipal as well as a moral and religious code; it contained many statutes ... of universal application—laws essential to the existence of men in society, and most of which have been enacted by every nation, which ever professed any code of laws. [9] JOHN QUINCY ADAMS

> The cultivation of the religious sentiment . . . inspires respect for law and order and gives strength to the whole social fabric. [10] DANIEL WEBSTER

> We have no government armed with power capable of contending with human passions unbridled by morality and religion. Avarice, ambition, revenge or gallantry would break the strongest cords of our Constitution as a whale goes through a net. Our Constitution was made only for a moral and religious people. It is wholly inadequate to the government of any other. [11] JOHN ADAMS

We have now set aside the sagacity and foresight of the Founders, and crime has exploded (see the following graph):

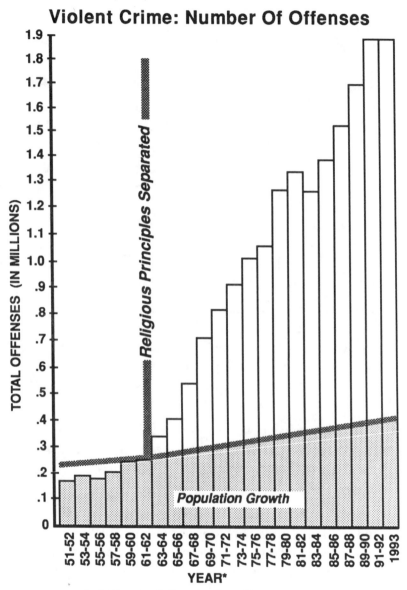

Violent Crime: Number Of Offenses

Religious Principles Separated

Population Growth

TOTAL OFFENSES (IN MILLIONS)

YEAR*

▨▨▨▨▨ Indicates population growth profile.

* Groupings represent average rate per year over the two-year period.

Basic data from *Statistical Abstracts of the United States*, and the Department of Commerce, Census Bureau.

Additionally:

- 57 million Americans—one in four—are annual victims of crime. [12]

- Theft against individual citizens costs $10.6 billion each year, and crimes against businesses cost at least $39.7 billion. [13]

- U. S. companies spend more than $4 billion a year for security, but still lose more than $7 billion a year to shoplifters. Consequently, stores must raise their prices as much as 15 percent to cover losses due to crime. [14]

- Crime costs U. S. citizens a total of $300 billion annually—an amount equal to almost 30 percent of the U. S. budget. If returned, that money could bring a windfall of $1,250 to every man, woman, and child in the country. [15]

- Between 1962 and 1993, the number of violent crimes increased 660 percent. [16]

Contrast this current condition with recent years when many individuals remember going to sleep at night with their back doors unlocked and their cars parked in the driveway with the keys left in the ignition.

Sexually Transmitted Diseases

As noted in earlier chapters, the Founders strongly warned that morality could not be maintained apart from religious principles. Early courts were just as poignant in their warnings:

> Christianity has reference to the principles of right and wrong . . . it is the foundation of those morals and manners upon which our society is formed. . . . The day of moral virtue in which we live would, in an instant, if that standard were abolished, lapse into the dark and murky night of Pagan immorality. [17] CITY OF CHARLESTON v. S. A. BENJAMIN

Such predictions of an inability to maintain national morality if religious principles were separated are now proven completely accurate: since the early 60s, there has been a national explosion of sexually-transmitted diseases (STDs). The current epidemic—there are now more than 25 different types of sexually-transmitted diseases—infects an average of 33,000 people a day. At this rate, one in four Americans between the ages of 15 and 55 eventually will acquire an STD. [18] In 1986 alone, there was a total of nearly 12 million new cases. [19] Additional statistics further document the dramatic explosion of STDs following the court-ordered removal of traditional religious and moral principles:

- Between 1965 and 1975, the cases of gonorrhea tripled, [20] and in 1984 alone, there were two million cases of gonorrhea and 90,000 cases of syphilis. [21]

- Between 1966 and 1984, genital herpes increased 1,500 percent, [22] now infecting 500,000 new victims annually. [23]

- Between 1966 and 1983, molluscum contagiosum (which causes lesions in the genital area) increased 1,100 percent. [24]

- Pelvic inflammatory disease (PID), a result of STDs, causes over 210,000 women to be hospitalized annually, [25] and the Center for Disease Control estimates that between 100,000 and 150,000 women are rendered sterile every year due to PID. [26]

- Chlamydia trachomatis—the fastest-growing and most common STD—infects four million annually and causes sterility in 11,000 women each year. [27]

- In 1984, there were an estimated one million new cases of genital warts—an STD linked to cancer. [28]

- STDs cost more than $2 billion annually in health-care. [29]

The effects of STDs are not limited solely to those who are active participants in promiscuous sexual relations; STDs in pregnant women have a secondary effect on the fetus and the newborn:

- Chlamydia in the mother causes lung and eye infections in newborns. [30]

- Venereal warts, transmitted to an infant during delivery, lodge in the larynx, trachea, and lungs. [31]

- Neonatal herpes frequently causes death or permanent neurological damage to the newborn. [32]

(Alcohol Use)

The evident loss of personal self-control following the separation of religious principles not only manifests itself in moral measurements but in a variety of others as well; for example, consider the skyrocketing problem of alcohol abuse. How large is the problem?

- Twenty-three million Americans (20 percent of whom are under the age of eighteen) have problems with alcohol; eighteen million take more than fourteen drinks per week; and twelve million suffer from alcoholism. [33]

- There were approximately three million alcohol-related arrests in 1992. [34]

- In 1985, more than nine out of ten high-school seniors used alcohol, [35] virtually all of whom were below the legal drinking age. [36]

- Among students, 45 percent of boys and 25 percent of girls are heavy-drinkers. [37]

- 437 students are arrested daily for drinking or for drunken driving. [38]

The direct effects from the increase in alcohol use are appalling:

- Each year, 100,000 people die from alcohol use, of which only one-fourth are traffic fatalities. [39]

- $116 billion is lost annually to alcohol abuse through missed days at work, insurance costs, etc. [40]

- Alcohol abuse contributes to skyrocketing medical health-care costs since it often results in numerous maladies, including ulcers, liver disease, pneumonia, cancers, etc. [41]

(*National Productivity*)

In the education section, it was noted that the rejection of religious principles, and thus of their associated teachings (i.e., self-control, respect, honesty, hard-work, etc.), created an environment producing substandard achievement. Since students carry their educational training and work-ethic into the work place, it is not surprising that business achievement is similarly affected.

National productivity, a measurement of the work preformed once students become adults and enter the work force, shows the same declines evidenced in the educational arena which prepared the students for their jobs. For example, a Department of Labor study comparing productivity among twelve manufacturing countries (the United States, Canada, Japan, France, Germany, Italy, United Kingdom, Belgium, Denmark, the Netherlands, Norway, and Sweden) revealed:

> Since 1960 . . . the United States shows the largest productivity decline. [42]

The effect on the U. S. economy of the persistent decline in productivity is substantial. Had the 1960 productivity rate continued, output by 1979 alone would have been at a level high enough to solve many of today's economic problems, most notably the budget deficit! [43] The following two graphs demonstrate the decline in productivity following the court-ordered change in educational policy.

Since the official exclusion of religion, this nation has undergone tremendous changes: violent crime offenses have risen nearly 700 percent; national productivity has dropped over 80 percent; cases of sexually transmitted diseases are up nearly 200 percent; and per capita alcohol consumption has increased by one-third.

Multi-Factor Productivity: Non-Farm Business

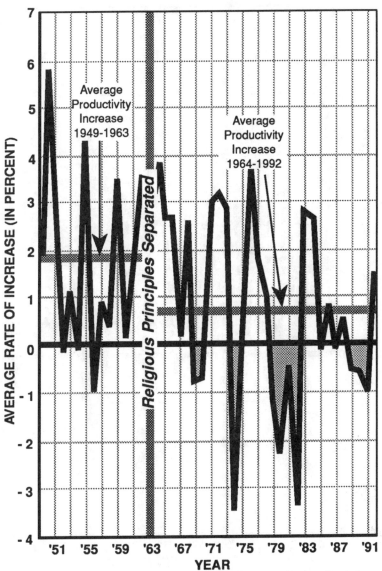

Basic data from Department of Labor, Bureau of Labor Statistics.

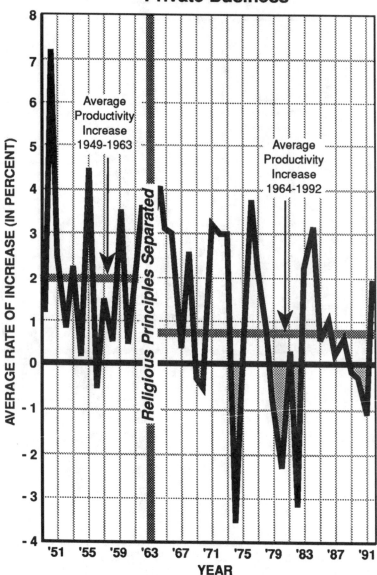

Multi-Factor Productivity: Private Business

Basic data from Department of Labor, Bureau of Labor Statistics.

(*Summary*)

The religion-related warnings given by Washington in his "Fare-well Address" are worthy of review:

- national morality cannot be maintained without religious principles;
- apart from religion, there will be no security for property or life;
- good policy finds its roots in religion and morality.

Washington concluded by asking:

> Who that is a sincere friend to it [American government] can look with indifference upon attempts to shake the foundation of the [national] fabric? [44]

Can a true friend to America remain indifferent to what has happened to America's foundation with the removal of religion and thus morality? Not in Washington's opinion.

Most national indicators of behavior show dramatic declines in personal self-control—those evident deficiencies of character by the removal of the religious teachings which produce personal self-control. Benjamin Franklin once sternly rebuked Thomas Paine who had attacked religion and asserted that good behavior could be maintained without religious teachings. Franklin reminded him:

> You yourself may find it easy to live a virtuous life without the assistance afforded by religion. . . . But think how great a portion of mankind consists of weak and ignorant men and women and of inexperienced, inconsiderate youth of both sexes who have need of the motives of religion to restrain them from vice, to support their virtue and retain them in the practice of it until it becomes habitual. . . . And perhaps you are indebted to her originally, that is, to your religion, education, for the habits of virtue upon which you now value yourself. . . . If men are so wicked with religion, what would they be if without it? [45]

Chapter 7
The Emergence of New National Problems

The problems which face America, both old and new, are documented in *Statistical Abstract of the United States,* an annual compilation of statistical data collected and tracked by various federal departments (Departments of Commerce, Labor, Health and Human Services, Justice, Education, etc.). Prior to 1962, categories tended to remain constant from year to year; however, since 1962, many new categories have emerged in the *Statistical Abstract.*

The appearance of a new statistical category is significant, for it indicates a sufficient national awareness of that problem to warrant its individual monitoring; in other words, a new category of statistics usually signals the identification of a new national problem. For example, statistics on child abuse first appeared in 1976. This does not mean that child abuse did not occur in previous years; it simply indicates that by 1976 it had become so widespread as to be considered a serious national problem.

Several of the new categories now monitored include:

- Child abuse (up 345 percent since 1976);

- Corruption of public officials (up nearly 500 percent since 1973);

- Illegal drug abuse (up 1,375 percent between 1962 and 1982);

- AIDs (an increase of over 97,000 percent increase in AIDS cases and 11,000 percent increase in AIDS deaths since 1981);

- Sexual abuse of children (up nearly 400 percent since 1976);

- Illiteracy (currently America has the highest illiteracy rate of any industrial nation).

Notice the escalation of these new categories:

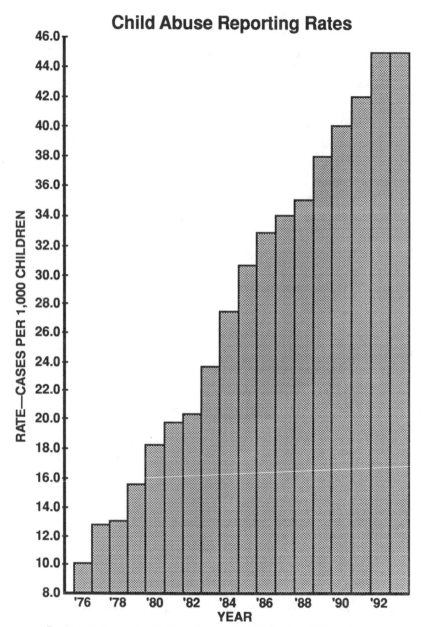

Child Abuse Reporting Rates

Basic data from *National Study on Child Neglect and Abuse Reporting*, annual. Provided by American Humane Association, Denver, CO.

Rate of Sexual Abuse of Children

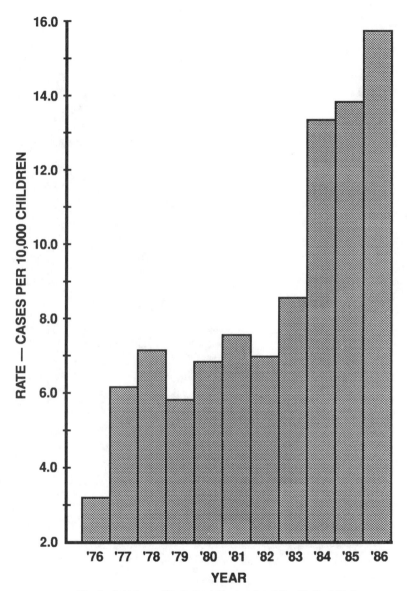

Basic data from *Statistical Abstracts of the United States.*

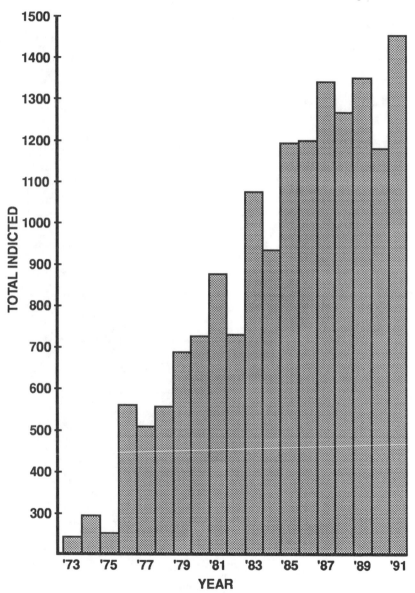

Federal Prosecutions of Public Corruption

Basic data from *Statistical Abstracts of the United States.*

AIDS

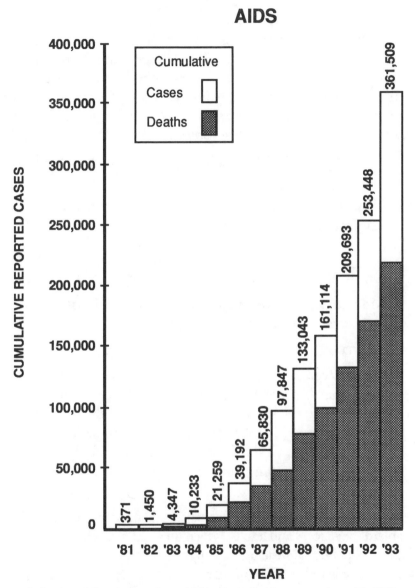

Collecting of data began June, 1981. Reporting began on June 15, 1982.

Basic data from *Aids Weekly Surveillance Report — United States*, Center for Disease Control.

(Drug Use)

According to the National Institute on Drug Abuse, America has a higher level of involvement with illegal drugs than any other industrialized nation in the world. [1] Nearly two-thirds of American teenagers have used drugs before they finish high school, and 40 percent have used drugs other than marijuana. [2] According to a survey entitled *Drugs and the Nation's High School Students:* [3]

- More than half of the high school students had tried marijuana;

- More than a quarter of the students reported using marijuana in the past month;

- One in six had used cocaine;

- One in eight had used hallucinogens such as LSD;

- Most students using drugs made their initial decision to try a drug between 7th and 10th grades.

Additionally:

A survey conducted by the Naval Health Research Center found that 48 percent of [military] recruits reported using marijuana in the six months before entering the service, and 42 percent said they "got drunk" at least once a week. . . . Last year . . . the United States decertified 1,400 people from handling nuclear weapons because of drug and alcohol abuse. [4]

In the "Gallup Youth Survey," teenagers said drug abuse is the largest problem they face, [5] and adults agreed: in a separate Gallup Poll, the American public said the use of drugs is the biggest problem facing public schools today. [6] The insulation of students from the religious principles which once taught absolutes has resulted in major deterioration in student beliefs of what constitutes right and wrong, as indicated on the following charts: [7]

Youth Who Have Ever Used Illegal Drugs

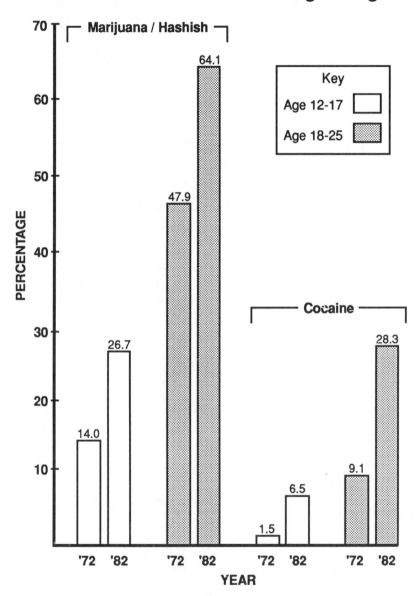

Basic data from *National Survey on Drug Abuse*,
provided by National Institute on Drug Abuse.

H.S. Seniors Who Had Tried Marijuana

59 %

4 %

1962   1982

University Of Michigan Survey, *Reader's Digest,* August 1983, p.138.

Illiteracy

According to the National Institute of Education:

- Up to 72 million American adults are functional illiterates (unable to read or write above the 5th-grade level), and 26 million cannot read or write at all. [8]

- Illiteracy rates run as high as 47 percent for 17-year-old minority youths, 60 percent for prison inmates, and 75 percent for unemployed people. [9]

- The number of adult illiterates is increasing by about 2.3 million each year. [10]

According to Project Literacy U. S. (PLUS):

- The U. S. has the highest illiteracy rate among industrial nations.

- Adult illiteracy costs the U. S. an estimated $225 billion yearly.

Functional illiterates commit many costly blunders. The Business Council for Effective Literacy in New York cites an insurance clerk who paid a claimant $2,200 on a $22 settlement because she didn't understand decimals; a steel-mill worker who misordered $1 million in parts because he could not read instructions well enough; a feedlot laborer who misread a label and killed a pen of cattle by giving them poison instead of feed. [11] While a high illiteracy rate might be expected in a third-world nation, it is unconscionable and unacceptable in the United States. Nevertheless, "the United States ranks 48th in adult literacy among the 149 countries represented at the United Nations," [12] the worst among industrial nations.

— — — • • • — — —

These are only a few of the many new national problems which have appeared since the change in national policy in 1962-63.

Chapter 8
National Accountability and
Biblical Repercussions

The United States has long been touted as a world leader. However, after significant declines in so many areas, one could properly question whether that claim is still justified. The resounding answer is "Yes!" although it is now in the wrong categories. Since 1962, the United States has become the world's leader in:

- Violent crime
- Divorce rate
- Teenage pregnancy rate (the western world's leader)
- Voluntary abortions
- Illegal drug use
- Illiteracy rate (the highest of any industrial nation)
- Documented cases of AIDS

Perhaps the best explanation for this reversal from our previous legacy was offered over 200 years ago by our Founding Fathers: the principle of rewards and punishments. The importance of this basic principle was so strongly embraced by them that it appeared throughout their official government documents. Notice:

And each member, before he takes his seat, shall make and subscribe the following declaration, viz: "I do believe in one God, the creator and governor of the universe, *the rewarder to the good and the punisher of the wicked.*" THE CONSTITUTIONS OF PENNSYLVANIA [1] AND VERMONT [2]

The qualifications of electors shall be [that he] . . . acknowledges the being of a God and *believes in the future states of rewards and punishments.* THE CONSTITUTION OF SOUTH CAROLINA [3]

> No person who denies the being of God, or *a future
> state of rewards and punishments,* shall hold any office
> in the civil department of this State. THE CONSTITUTION
> OF TENNESSEE [4]

Many additional documents affirm the Founders' strong belief that each individual would one day stand before God Almighty, first to account for his actions, then to receive the dispensing of rewards or punishments. Yet the Founders' writings reveal that their understanding of accountability to God was not limited solely to individual behavior; it also encompassed national behavior. They understood the clear Biblical differences between those two.

An individual's final reckoning with God will occur after his departure from this life; perhaps immediately after death or 10,000 years later, but it will occur; a final future reckoning is inevitable. [5] However, a nation, unlike an individual, does not account to God in the future. As explained by George Mason on the floor of the Constitutional Convention, nations account to God in the present:

> As nations cannot be rewarded or punished in the next
> world, so they must be in this. By an inevitable chain of
> causes and effects, Providence punishes national sins by
> national calamities. [6]

It is this explanation which has so much potential in explaining what has occurred to this nation since 1962. God responds now to what a nation does now; He responds to nations in the present. The Bible is filled with accounts confirming this truth.

Consider Elijah's conflict with the prophets of Baal on Mt. Carmel (1 Kings 18). Following his victory and the complete vindication of God, Elijah retreated to Mt. Horeb where he complained to God that he was the only righteous individual left in the nation. God promptly informed him that, no, he was not; there were still 7,000 righteous men of integrity in the nation who had never bowed their knees to Baal. Yet these 7,000 righteous men, as was the case with every other individual in the nation, had just suffered through a three-

and-a-half-year famine imposed by God on that nation because of the wicked stands taken by the nation's leaders, Ahab and Jezebel. God judged the entire nation based on the actions and stands taken by its leaders. Another instance of national accountability occurred when King David numbered his troops (1 Chronicles 21). David's act was based on his assumption that the size of his army was responsible for his many victories. Gloating in his own strength and military accomplishments, David forgot that the reason for his many victories had been God's direct aid (see Isaiah 10:12b-16a and Proverbs 21:31). Benjamin Franklin's reminder on the floor of the Constitutional Convention in 1787 would have been useful to King David:

> In the beginning of the contest with Great Britain, when we were sensible of danger, we had daily prayer in this room for the Divine protection. —Our prayers, Sir, were heard, and they were graciously answered. All of us who were engaged in the struggle must have observed frequent instances of a superintending Providence in our favor . . . And have we now forgotten this powerful Friend? Or do we imagine we no longer need His assistance? [7]

When General Joab tried to dissuade David from his foolhardy show of self-reliance by numbering his troops (1 Chronicles 21:3), David ignored Joab's advice and ordered the count to be made. David's official stand rejected any acknowledgment of God or of His hand, and consequently a plague befell the nation (1 Chronicles 21:14). Once again, the stand taken by a nation's leader, and God's corresponding response to that stand, affected the entire nation.

Not only George Mason and Benjamin Franklin expressed their understanding of this principle of accountability, but Thomas Jefferson, when discussing the wrongs of slavery and slave ownership, recognized the same truth. His statement on national accountability to God was so important that it was engraved inside the Jefferson Memorial in Washington. Jefferson forcefully declared:

Indeed, I tremble for my country when I reflect that God is just and that His justice cannot sleep forever. [8]

President Lincoln, too, understood national accountability to God. Once, on overhearing a clergyman say that he hoped "the Lord was on our side," Lincoln replied:

I am not at all concerned about that, for I know that the Lord is always on the side of the right. But it is my constant anxiety and prayer that I and this nation should be on the Lord's side. [9]

It is vital that a nation's leaders take stands which cause God to remain an ally to that nation and not to become its enemy. Is it simply coincidence that each of the categories presented in this book began to deteriorate visibly and dramatically immediately after the nation's leaders repudiated God and His principles? Or can it be that the principle of national accountability is at work?

The simple acknowledgment of God has provided us with more blessings and prosperity than we can comprehend. The Bible clearly records God's promise: "Whoever honors me, I will honor. And whoever disregards me, I will disregard" (1 Samuel 2:30). When we were honoring God in our public affairs, we were elevated among the nations of the world in achievement, morality, productivity, stability, and reputation. Since disregarding Him, we are no longer the same superior nation; our performances have lapsed into mediocrity. As noted by the Department of Education:

The educational foundations of our society are presently being eroded by a rising tide of mediocrity that threatens our very future as a Nation and a People. . . . If an unfriendly power had attempted to impose on America the mediocre educational performance that exists today, we might well have viewed it as an act of war. As it stands, we have allowed this to happen to ourselves. [10]

Psalms 91:14-16 holds forth a powerful promise to nations as well as individuals. In these verses, God declares:

> I will protect him, for he acknowledges My name. He will call upon Me, and I will answer him; I will be with him in trouble; I will deliver him and honor him; with long life will I satisfy him, and show him My salvation.

Notice the benefits of openly acknowledging God—benefits enjoyed by this nation prior to 1962:

- *"I will protect him . . ."* The remarkably low rates of crime, abuse, pregnancies, STDs, etc. evidence that we definitely were under Divine protection and blessing.

- *"I will answer him . . ."* Statistics on students, families, schools, and the nation demonstrated extraordinary stability.

- *"I will be with him in trouble . . ."* We experienced low divorce rates and fewer family breakups.

- *"I will honor him . . ."* We enjoyed a lofty international reputation.

- *"With long life will I satisfy him . . ."* Suicide rates were low among students, as was loss of life by murder and deaths caused by sexually transmitted diseases.

Jeremiah 8 specifically elucidates the problems which occur when a nation rejects God in the manner done by our Court in 1962-63:

> Since they have rejected the word of the Lord, what kind of wisdom do they have? Therefore I will give their wives to other men and their fields to new owners . . . They dress the wound of my people as though it were not serious, saying "Peace, peace" when there is no peace . . . they have no shame at all; they do not even know how to blush. So they will fall among the fallen . . . I will take away their harvest, there will be no figs on the tree, and their leaves will wither. What I have given them will be taken away.

Notice the accuracy of these verses:

- *"Since they have rejected the word of the Lord, what kind of wisdom do they have?"* Our academic achievements have plummeted both in domestic and international testing.

- *"Therefore I will give their wives to other men . . ."* Adultery has risen three to four times its previous level, and divorce and remarriage have skyrocketed, as have unmarried couples living together.

- *". . . and their fields to new owners . . ."* Defaults on payments and subsequent repossession of property has skyrocketed, with 875,000 bankruptcies in 1993 alone. [11]

- *"They dress the wound of my people as though it were not serious, saying 'Peace, peace' when there is no peace . . ."* Our nation downplays the enormity of its problems and attempts merely to treat the symptoms of serious problems such as illiteracy, poor academic achievement, STDs, etc., while ignoring the root causes.

- *"They have no shame at all; they do not even know how to blush . . ."* Morality is a word with new parameters: things previously done only in secret—and never discussed—are now done openly with little or no embarrassment. Now, when speaking of "gay" clothing or a "gay" party, one no longer means "jolly and happy" but describes an entire subculture based on immoral behavior.

- *"So they will fall among the fallen . . ."* Our international positions in education, industry, morality, and family stability have fallen to the worst levels of any industrial nation.

- *"I will take away their harvest, there will be no figs on the tree, and their leaves will wither . . ."* Our productivity has dropped almost 80 percent from its pre-1962 levels.

- *"What I have given them will be taken away . . ."* Major reversals have occurred in numerous national areas since God and His principles were barred from public affairs. We have become a nation embarrassed by its educational system, public corruption, illiteracy, immorality, child abuse, and drug use.

When contemplating His treatment by the nation's leaders, God asks a probing question in Jeremiah 7:

> Am I the one they are provoking? Are they not rather harming themselves to their own shame?

Obviously, our prohibition of Christian principles in public affairs did nothing to harm God, but it certainly has scandalized the entire nation. The words of Franklin's admonition again come to mind:

> Without His concurring aid . . . we ourselves shall become
> a reproach and a byword down to future ages. [12]

The practice of public prayer and of seeking God's "concurring aid" was integral to this nation's birth, growth, development, and maturing. We were born and guided through our adolescence and then brought through turmoil and on to stability by men who embraced prayer and religious principles. Can we possibly believe that what was gained by those principles can be maintained without them?

As suggested by the graphs and statistics, prayer in schools and the acknowledgment of God throughout public affairs is not simply a religious issue; it is a vital national issue. Obtaining God's aid and favor by simply acknowledging Him in public is an asset not to be underestimated, and we can ill afford to continue without His aid and favor. Hosea 6:3 needs again to become the description of our national policy:

> "Let us press on to acknowledge Him."

Chapter 9
Strategy For a Change

What can be done to halt the havoc loosed on the nation since the early 60s? To recover from the effects of the Court's rulings, there must be two reversals. The first and most obvious one must occur in our national public stance toward God: the Court's current ban on the acknowledgment of God and the use of His principles in public is a direct challenge to Him and has thus triggered the law of national accountability, subjecting the nation to severe consequences. Therefore, our current national public stand against God must be set aside.

The second reversal must center on the restoration of the personal benefits derived from living by Godly principles. For example, when the Courts ruled that students might not use the Ten Commandments, nor study the Scriptures, nor learn about sexual abstinence, etc., the separation of these teachings caused personal, individual harm to those students, as forewarned in Deuteronomy 6:24 and 10:13:

> The Lord commanded us to obey all these decrees *so that we might always prosper.*
>
> Observe the Lord's decrees *for your own good.*

Observing His principles serves to *our* benefit. When His commands are rejected, it is to our own harm. As already demonstrated, millions have been harmed by the mandated separation of His principles from specific arenas of their lives. The efforts at restoration and reversal must occur on both the national and on the individual levels.

However, before attempting any change at the national level, it is first imperative to understand what caused contemporary courts to rule as they did. Not understanding the causes which opened the door for such rulings would be an invitation to future repetitions of what began in 1962.

Consider: how was it possible that in 1962 when the official public acknowledgment of God was eliminated from schools that 97 percent of the nation claimed a belief in God? [1] While some of the blame may be laid at the feet of the Court's "Doctrine of Separation" which now dominates its rulings, most of the blame must properly be laid at the feet of the Christian community-at-large.

In the decades immediately preceding the Court rulings (the 1920s, 30s, 40s, etc.), Christians *en masse* had voluntarily removed themselves from the political, social, and legal arenas. Whenever the Godly depart from any arena, their own Godly values depart with them. That arena is then refilled by the unGodly, and it should come as no surprise that their rulings and public policies would reflect their own personal unGodly values. A person in office always legislates according to *his own* personal beliefs and convictions, and herein is the wisdom of Proverbs 29:2 made evident: "When the righteous rule, the people rejoice; when the wicked rule, the people groan." The following excerpts from constitutions authored by the Founding Fathers confirm their understanding of the principle expressed in Proverbs 29:2. Notice:

> [Everyone appointed to public office must say]: "I . . . do profess faith in God the Father, and in Jesus Christ His only Son, and in the Holy Ghost, one God, blessed for evermore; and I do acknowledge the Holy Scriptures of the Old and New Testament to be given by Divine inspiration." DELAWARE CONSTITUTION, 1776 [2]

> And each member [of the legislature], before he takes his seat, shall make and subscribe the following declaration, viz: "I do believe in one God, the Creator and Governor of the universe, the rewarder of the good and the punisher of the wicked, and I do acknowledge the Scriptures of the Old and New Testament to be given by Divine Inspiration." PENNSYLVANIA CONSTITUTION, 1776 [3]

> [All persons elected must] make and subscribe the following declaration, viz: "I do declare that I believe the Christian religion and have firm persuasion of its truth." MASSACHUSETTS CONSTITUTION, 1780 [4]

These excerpts were not isolated portions of obscure laws, nor were they "mistakes." These laws remained in force for years after the ratification of the Constitution, and the U. S. Supreme Court even cited them as proof of the Founders' intent. [5] It was the plan and intent of the Founders that the Godly, and thereby Godly principles, remain intimately involved in the political, judicial, and educational realms. The Founders believed that only the Godly would understand the unalienable freedoms provided by God and thus protect them in our form of government.

The major religious concern which the Founders expressed during the drafting of the First Amendment was their desire to prevent any single denomination from ruling the nation, as had occurred in Great Britain. The Founders intended to prohibit the federal government from declaring the entire nation to be *only* Catholic, *only* Baptist, *only* Methodist, etc. Consequently, the First Amendment simply stated:

> Congress shall make no law regarding the establishment
> of religion or prohibiting the free exercise thereof.

The words "separation," "church," or "state" do not even appear in the First Amendment, and the Founders *never* intended that Christian principles be divorced from public affairs. Unfortunately, we forgot this; the danger of forgetting is well expressed by President Woodrow Wilson:

> A nation which does not remember what it was yesterday,
> does not know what it is today, nor what it is trying to do.
> We are trying to do a futile thing if we do not know where
> we came from or what we have been about. [6]

By forgetting not only our heritage but also the Biblical truth of Proverbs 29:2, we began to extract ourselves from public affairs. Many Christians leaders, while encouraging young people to become pastors or missionaries, discouraged them from entering the legal, political, or public arenas. Little by little, the church-at-large not only embraced but even began to teach the heresy that Christians and politics were incompatible and should be divorced.

Through this slow but steady process, Christians gradually—and voluntarily—relinquished their political and judicial positions. The Godly withdrew from these arenas and their replacements were not Godly nor did they hold precious the beliefs that had shaped and guided the nation for almost two centuries. Not surprisingly, they began to introduce new ideas and laws which, although consistent with their own personal beliefs, were contrary to our heritage and values.

The church was so entrenched in its self-imposed isolation that it took little action to stop them. This seclusion not only insulted our heritage, it was a Biblical error:

> He who isolates himself seeks his own selfish desires; he rages against all sound judgment. PROVERBS 18:1

Christians, through bad doctrine, political inactivity, and apathy had handed the reins of the nation over to leaders who awarded lifelong appointments to Justices not only willing but also eager to uproot the Christian practices that had been the heart of this nation for centuries. Quite frankly, the Court's 1962 (and subsequent) decisions were merely an outgrowth of what the Christian community-at-large had permitted and encouraged in the decades preceding those rulings.

A Biblical description of this process is given by Jesus in Matthew 13:24-26. In that parable, good people had a good field growing good seed. However, an enemy came in and planted bad among the good, thus contaminating the entire field. What afforded the enemy such an opportunity? The stark answer is found in verse 24: "While the good men slept, the enemy came in." Jesus never faulted the enemy for doing what he did, for it was his task and purpose to destroy; Jesus placed the fault on the good men who went to sleep, thus allowing the enemy to do what he did. Very bluntly what has occurred in America happened *first* because the church went to sleep, and *then* because the enemy came in and caused the damage.

Having by our own abdication transferred a nation built on Godly principles into the hands of unGodly men, should we really be surprised by what has happened? Yet there still remains great hope and cause for optimism.

Chapter 10
What Can Be Done Now?

The problems we have created for ourselves, although colossal, can be solved. Reversing the current trends involves making changes in the two areas mentioned earlier: (1) the official unfriendly stand taken against God must be corrected, and (2) religious principles and moral teachings must be restored and made available to individuals in public arenas. There are at least ten specific activities suggested in this chapter which can help realize these goals.

[1] The first thing is to do first things first:

> I exhort therefore, that, *first of all*, supplications, prayers, intercessions, and giving of thanks, be made for all men, for [leaders] and for all that are in authority. 1 TIMOTHY 2:1

This is not an arbitrary, haphazard plan given by God; God wants every individual to pray for civic leaders *first*, because civic leaders and their policies affect every individual. Simply for our own benefit we should be praying regularly for our leaders at local, state, and federal levels in each branch of government. Prayer will be the first key to effecting significant and lasting change, for situations do not change on earth until they have been changed in the heavenlies. As Jesus taught: "*Thy* Kingdom come, *Thy* will be done, *on earth as it is in Heaven.*"

Additionally, we need to pray faithfully that God will root the wicked from office and will raise up righteous individuals to replace them. "An ounce of prevention is worth a pound of cure," and having the right individuals in office will prevent the enactment of many damaging policies. As explained by William Penn:

> [G]overnments rather depend upon men than men upon governments. . . . Let men be good and the government cannot be bad. . . . [T]hough good laws do well, good men do better; for good laws may want [lack] good men . . . but good men will never want [lack] good laws nor suffer [allow bad] ill ones. [1]

Pray individually not only for our leaders on every level, but enlarge your sphere of influence and organize small groups to pray for our leaders. *Item #1—Become active in praying for leaders and officials at all levels.*

• • •

2 Voluntary prayer currently is greatly restricted in many schools, but that does not mean children should not be trained daily to pray. If you have children of school age, pray with them each day before they leave for school. Show them from the Scriptures the importance of prayer and petition, and help them begin each day by seeking God. Encourage them to pray specifically for students, families, schools, and the nation. God wants us to train our children in the importance of prayer.

The prayer of the upright is His delight. PROVERBS 15:8
Pray without ceasing. 1 THESSALONIANS 5:17
Continue in prayer. COLOSSIANS 4:2

Item #2—Become active in praying with your children.

• • •

3 Children currently receive little accurate information from their schools or public institutions either about the historical role of Christians in the nation or about the importance of involving Godly principles in our public affairs. Nevertheless, you can help them obtain correct information.

If you have children, teach them the Christian history, heritage, and traditions of our nation, and help them to recognize that the current "Doctrine of Separation" is hostile toward Christianity, that it is unfounded, and that it is wrong.

If you do not have children, then educate those around you (i.e., Sunday School class, civic club, etc.) to an accurate history of our nation. (A list of recommended reading/resource books containing accurate history is included in Appendix B.) *Item #3—Become active in teaching the truth to others.*

•   •   •

[4] The political realm, formerly dominated by Christians, is still available to them. It was the use of politics that resulted in the elimination of religious activities and the public acknowledgment of God from public affairs; it can therefore restore those principles. While it might seem easier to empty the ocean with a thimble than to change politics, it is actually not as difficult as many people think.

Just as Christians have improperly believed that we must isolate ourselves from politics, we have also incorrectly believed that we don't have the power to change politics. We've probably heard, or perhaps even made, statements such as: "I'm only an individual—one vote. What can I do?" "My vote won't make a difference anyway." "It does us no good to vote. As Christians, we're already in the minority." Sound familiar? The fact is, such statements are *not* true.

A recent Gallup Poll shows that 84 percent of this nation firmly believe in Jesus Christ, [2] and a separate poll indicates that 94 percent believe in God. [3] Polls have shown that:

- Over 80 percent approve of voluntary prayer in school. [4]

- 81 percent of the nation opposes special rights for homosexuals. [5]

- 89 percent opposes the use of abortion as a means of convenience birth control. [6]

Additional findings could be cited, but the conclusion is inescapable: although we have been led to believe that we, the 94 percent who believe in God, are the minority, we most definitely are not!

The Constitution makes it clear that numbers are important. This is to be a government of a majority of the people, by the majority of the people, and for a majority of the people. Imagine a hypothetical vote in the U. S. Senate where the final tally was 94 to 6. It would be untenable for the 6 to be declared the winner and to have their policy enacted over the votes of the 94; yet this is exactly what happened when the public acknowledgment of God was prohibited. Can such an act truly be appropriate either in a republic (to which we pledge our allegiance) or in a democracy (which we most often claim to be)? Certainly not! Yet, unfortunately, this travesty continues to occur on a regular basis today. We have relinquished our right to be a democratic-republic and instead have become an oligarchy—a nation ruled by a small group or a council of "elite" individuals.

While polls show that the overwhelming majority of our citizens seem ready to return Godly precepts to public affairs, it is clear that a vast number of our elected officials are not. Whose fault is that? Notice President James Garfield's answer to this question:

> Now, more than ever before, the people are responsible for the character of their Congress. If that body be ignorant, reckless, and corrupt, it is because the people tolerate ignorance, recklessness, and corruption. If it be intelligent, brave, and pure, it is because the people demand these high qualities to represent them in the national legislature. . . . If the next centennial does not find us a great nation . . . it will be because those who represent the enterprise, the culture, and the morality of the nation do not aid in controlling the political forces. [7]

If we want different national policies, it is up to *us*, the citizens, not *them*, the leaders.

Proof of this came in five separate U. S. Senate races in 1986. The five candidates who stood for returning Godly principles to public affairs were defeated by a collective total of only 57,000 votes—less than 12,000 votes per state. Yet in those five states, there were *over 5 million Christians* who did not even vote! If only 1 of every 100 *non-voting Christians*—one percent—had voted for the candidate supporting Godly principles, those five would have been elected and would have created a ten-vote swing in the Senate; five unGodly men would have been retired and five Godly men would have taken their places.

This is not the disheartening report it seems; actually, it is very encouraging, for it shows that Godly candidates are most often defeated not by activists and radicals, but by inactive Christians! This means that we *do* have the power to make a difference. When Christians begin to believe that we can make a difference and begin to act like the majority we are, we *will* make a difference. The ability to change the current situation is in *our* hands. As Edward Burke explained:

> All that is necessary for evil to triumph is for good men to do nothing. [8]

There is much that "good men" can do to stop the triumph of evil. One of the most important is to vote, and to vote Biblically. John Jay, America's first Chief Justice of the Supreme Court, once received a letter inquiring from him whether it was permissible for a Christian to vote for an unGodly candidate. Jay responded:

> Whether our religion permits Christians to vote for infidel rulers is a question which merits more consideration than it seems yet to have generally received either from the clergy or the laity. It appears to me that what the prophet said to Jehoshaphat about his attachment to Ahab ["Shouldest thou help the ungodly and love them that hate the Lord?" 2 Chronicles 19:2] affords a salutary lesson. [9]

On another occasion, Jay advised:

> Providence has given to our people the choice of their rulers. It is the *duty,* as well as the privilege and interest, of our Christian nation to select and prefer Christians for their rulers. [10]

Daniel Webster delivered a similarly strong warning to teach our youth that:

> [T]he exercise of the elective franchise is a social duty of as solemn a nature as man can be called to perform; that a man may not innocently trifle with his vote; that every

free elector is a trustee as well for others as himself; and that every man and every measure he supports has an important bearing on the interests of others as well as on his own. [11]

Founding Father Noah Webster delivered a similar admonition:

Let it be impressed on your mind that God commands you to choose for rulers just men who will rule in the fear of God [Exodus 18:21]. . . . [I]f the citizens neglect their duty and place unprincipled men in office, the government will soon be corrupted . . . If [our] government fails to secure public prosperity and happiness, it must be because the citizens neglect the Divine commands, and elect bad men to make and administer the laws. [12]

These admonitions to vote, and to vote Biblically, came not only from our political leaders, but from our spiritual leaders as well. Charles Finney, a prominent minister in the early 1800s, succinctly declared:

The time has come that Christians must vote for honest men and take consistent ground in politics or the Lord will curse them. . . . God cannot sustain this free and blessed country which we love and pray for unless the Church will take right ground. [13]

The dilemma now facing us as Christians is similar to that faced by a group in the Bible who, like us today, were experiencing severe national problems affecting their personal lives. As those individuals contemplated their course of action, they concluded (as should we) that involvement was the only reasonable alternative. As they so aptly quipped in 2 Kings 7:3:

Why sit we here 'til we die?

It is time to believe and to behave differently. We are *not* a minority; we *are* the majority! It is time to declare at the ballot box that we will no longer allow officials who embrace the values of the 6 percent who do not believe in God to abrogate the rights of the 94 percent who do. We must remove officials who do not comply with traditional, historical, and Biblical principles and replace them with those who do. We *can* make a difference! Our vote *does* count! *Item #4— Become an active voter.*

• • •

5 Too often, an allegedly "good" candidate is elected and we later end up regretting his public stands and votes. Much of this could be eliminated if the right questions were asked *before* election. We need to know more about a candidate than just the professional qualifications; we also need to know the *personal* traits that qualify him to represent us. As pointed out in a famous textbook first published in 1800:

> A public character is often an artificial one. It is not, then, in the glare of public, but in the shade of private life that we are to look for the man. Private life is always real life. Behind the curtain, where the eyes of the million are not upon him ... there he will always be sure to act himself: consequently, if he act greatly, he must be great indeed. Hence it has been justly said, that, "our private deeds, if noble, are noblest of our lives." ... [I]t is the private virtues that lay the foundation of all human excellence. [14]

It is not only proper, it is vital to investigate a candidate's *private* life and beliefs *before* placing him into office. The reason is made clear in Matthew 7:16-20 and in Luke 6:43-44; in these passages, Jesus reminds us that bad roots *will* produce bad fruit. Consequently, a candidate's moral and religious "roots" must be investigated before placing him into office. A candidate who produced bad fruit in private life *will* produce bad fruit in public life. Understanding this truth, Founding Father Elias Boudinot, President of the Continental Congress, reminded us to ...

> ... be religiously careful in our choice of all public officers ... and judge of the tree by its fruits. [15]

John Adams similarly charged us:

> We electors have an important constitutional power placed
> in our hands; we have a check upon two branches of the
> legislature. . . . It becomes necessary to every [citizen] then,
> to be in some degree a statesman: and to examine and judge
> for himself . . . the . . . political principles and measures.
> Let us examine, then, with a sober . . . Christian spirit. [16]

While there are many ways to ascertain a candidate's private beliefs and behavior, two are readily available to any individual or group.
The first is outside monitoring, and the second is direct questioning.

OUTSIDE MONITORING. Many groups publish a voter's guide showing
the voting records of incumbents and the position of challengers on
moral and religious issues of concern to the God-fearing community. A listing of several of these groups may be found in Appendix
A. Contact the group's national headquarters to get information on
obtaining a voter's guide for your state. The national group will usually refer you to one of their state groups/chapters in your local area.
While each of the national groups may not have a representative,
there is usually at least one of the groups which *will* have a contact in
your area. You may have to call several of the national groups before
you finally make the local connection you need, but don't give up; the
information you finally receive will be well worth the effort.

DIRECT QUESTIONING. Another way to obtain information on a candidate's stands on specific issues is simply to phone his or her office
and ask. In addition to any questions which you might have concerning state or local issues, three additional questions you can pose will
almost universally reveal the moral philosophy which guides that candidate. Specifically question each candidate on:

- His view on the relationship between God and
  government.

- His view on abortion.

- His view on homosexual behavior.

The answers to these questions will reveal whether the candidate perceives the importance of God's principles to government, whether he understands the value of life and of protecting the innocent, and finally whether he believes that there are behavioral absolutes based on fundamental rights and wrongs. How a candidate answers these three questions will identify the moral foundation from which all other political decisions will be made.

No matter which position a candidate is seeking, scrutinize his stands. Some candidates will argue that since they are seeking only the position of justice-of-the-peace, city-treasurer, dogcatcher, etc., that their stands on issues like abortion will have no bearing on their office. While that statement may seem innocuous, it is misleading.

In Exodus 18:21, God holds forth the same standards for *all* elected officials regardless of whether they are "leaders of tens" (local), "leaders of fifties" (county), "leaders of hundreds" (state), or "leaders of thousands" (federal). The logic behind this is simple: nearly every current "leader of thousands" was once a "leader of tens"; that is, many low-level local offices have been starting points for prominent national careers. Therefore, screen candidates thoroughly at the lowest levels of government, for this is where their election or defeat is the easiest. Once a candidate is in office and becomes an incumbent, statistics show that his defeat and removal from office is much more difficult.

When you examine a candidate, realize that it is not vital that you agree on every specific doctrinal point. The determining factor is, do we agree on what the Founding Fathers called "the moral law"?; that is, do we agree on the moral essentials? Alexis de Tocqueville, in his famous book *Democracy in America* (still available in bookstores today), explained:

> The sects [Christian denominations] which exist in the United States are innumerable. They all differ in respect to the worship which is due from man to his Creator; but they all agree in respect to the duties which are due from man to man. Each sect adores the Deity in its own peculiar manner; but all the sects preach the same moral law in

the name of God . . . [A]lmost all the sects of the United
States are comprised within the great unity of Christianity,
and Christian morality is everywhere the same. [17]

This nation will not be put back on track by Baptists alone, or by
Catholics alone, or by Methodists alone, or by Pentecostals alone, or
by any other single group; there is not enough strength in any one
denomination to return America to its Biblical roots. However, it
will be put back on track by Christians of all denominations committed to the same moral law of God. Be prepared to accommodate
an appropriate degree of tolerance for those of other religious com-
munities without compromising basic Biblical principles of morality.

Once you have determined each candidate's stand on moral and
religious issues, do all you can to publicize those positions to your
friends, acquaintances, and associates. *Item #5—Become active in
investigating and publicizing the stands of candidates.*

(Note: It does not violate any tax-exempt provision of the IRS for
a church to distribute voter's guides or candidate positions; a voter's
guide is an educational publication and does not jeopardize a church's
tax-exempt status. A church may educate its members on the beliefs
of candidates concerning issues of concern to Christians. It is only
as an official corporate body that the church may not endorse a specific candidate or party. However, a pastor may endorse a candidate
or a party—even from the pulpit—as long as he makes it clear that
he is simply delivering his own opinion and that he is not speaking
on behalf of the church board or church corporation. A pastor does
not forfeit his right to freedom of speech just because he is a pastor.)

• • •

6 After you have identified a Godly candidate, there is much you
can do to help him. Frequently such a candidate may not receive
good media coverage; however, this is neither an unusual nor an in-
surmountable problem. Candidates with strong grass-roots efforts
regularly overcome the media influence and win.

Once you identify a candidate who can make a positive difference, get involved with him. Offer as much financial support as you can (whether little or much), and then call the office and volunteer some time to the campaign, even if it is only an hour or two. By volunteering to help a Godly candidate, you will, in fact, be helping yourself and your posterity; it is important to remember posterity and to leave them something better than we have. The Rev. Matthias Burnet, in a sermon delivered before the Connecticut legislature in 1803, addressed this very concern when he stated:

> Finally, ye . . . whose high prerogative it is to . . . invest with office and authority or to withhold them, [by voting] and in whose power it is to save or destroy your country, consider well the important trust . . which God . . . [has] put into your hands. To God and posterity you are accountable for them. . . . *Let not your children have reason to curse you for giving up those rights and prostrating those institutions which your fathers delivered to you.* [18]

We need to help the good candidates, for our own sake and for the sake of our children. However, when helping a candidate, learn to look beyond party. You might have been born a Democrat; you might have been born a Republican; you might have been born an Independent; that doesn't matter. The fact is, you were reborn a Christian; reflect that in your political involvement. As Founding Father Benjamin Rush once declared:

> I have been alternately called an aristocrat and a democrat. I am neither. I am a Christocrat. I believe all power . . . will always fail of producing order and happiness in the hands of man. He alone who created and redeemed man is qualified to govern him. [19]

Be a Christocrat; get involved with solid Godly candidates no matter what their party. *Item #6—Become active in helping candidates.*

• • •

7 Another mechanism for effective change is direct contact with your Congressman. A sincere, personal letter expressing your views and your concerns to your Congressman *is* effective, but for too long, most Americans have underestimated the effect they can have and thus have remained silent on many issues.

In June 1989, I had opportunity to participate directly in the introduction of a significant federal legislative bill. The bill received support from a wide variety of Congressmen (in fact, in the preceding month, the House of Representatives had voted two-to-one in favor of the material in the proposed bill). The bill was referred to the appropriate committee and subcommittee; however, those two chairmen refused to allow any hearings or discussion on the bill; they were both determined to let it die in committee.

Because of the widespread support already evident, and because it seemed inappropriate for only two individuals to block the progress of that bill, we asked several Congressmen how to get that bill released from the committee. The Congressmen instructed us to locate individuals in those two men's home districts who would be willing to write letters to the two requesting that the bill be released and that hearings be scheduled on it.

To determine how many letters would be needed, we queried several: "Congressman, how do you know when you have a 'hot' issue?" Their answer was startling: "If we get as many as fifty letters on a bill, it's a very hot issue." They further indicated that, in their opinion, twenty letters would be sufficient pressure to cause the two Congressmen to reverse their position on the bottled-up bill. Amazed, we asked: "How many letters do you usually receive on a bill?" They responded, "Five to ten is normal."

The fact that five to ten letters is the norm on a bill is a compelling commentary on the inactivity of most of us. Each Congressman represents at least 500,000 individuals, and as few as 20 letters can cause him to reverse his stand! This explains why philosophical minorities and anti-Christian groups are often more successful in reaching their goals in Congress: they are simply more active in generating individual contacts with a Congressman.

Another similar account comes from a U. S. Congressman in a northwestern state. In 1990, during the closing weeks of the 101st Congress, one of the especially "hot" items was the federal budget. There had been numerous stalemates in negotiations between Congress and the White House, and several volatile proposals were offered for cutting the budget—proposals ranging from raising taxes to cutting Social Security, Medicare, salaries of federal workers, etc. (all items particularly sensitive to large portions of the nation and issues which produced open wrath and hostility from many segments of the public).

That Congressman's staff knew that the budget negotiations were a "hot" item due to the number of constituent phone calls which he claimed had "poured" into his office over a five-week period. How many calls had "poured in" during those five weeks? Six!—His office had received a total of *six calls* about the budget, thus convincing him that this was a "hot" issue to his constituents! When a legislator is accustomed to receiving little or no communication from constituents on most issues, six calls can indeed seem like a flood.

In communicating with your Congressman, it is important that your contacts be personal. Congressmen openly acknowledge that mass-produced mailings, form letters, or petitions get no response and usually go into the trash. In their view, if a person does not feel strongly enough about a bill or an issue to express himself in a personal, original letter, then he receives little serious consideration.

A personal letter *is* effective, even a short one; and letter writing is not only easy, but often takes less time than imagined. Usually, the difficulty is simply in getting started; once you begin your letter, the thoughts and feelings flow easily. Here are a few suggestions to assist you in effective letter writing:

- Be personal in your letter. Use the name of your Congressman—*don't* address it to "Dear Congressman". You typically don't appreciate mail addressed to "Dear Occupant"; neither does he; call him/her by name. (You can obtain the name of your Congressman through the library, Chamber of Commerce, or other similar public service organizations.)

- Get to the point—don't be long-winded or wordy; three or four paragraphs is plenty and is much more likely to receive serious attention than is a lengthy letter. After a short friendly greeting, explain why you are writing and what you would like the Congressman to do.

- Be specific in your requests. If possible, try to give the name, number, or description of the bill or measure with which you are concerned. Do *not* ask him to do general things like bring world peace, end the famines in Africa, etc.; he can no more do that than you can.

- Don't get preachy. Give practical, well-thought-out, logical reasons for your position and why you want him to take certain steps. Don't use Christian clichés or phrases.

- Don't threaten. Don't tell him, for example, that if he doesn't vote the way you want that you will never vote for him again, or that if he doesn't stop abortion that he will stand before God and answer for his votes. Although these things may be true, Philippians 2:14 instructs us to do everything without threatening. Threats tend to bring out the stubborn side in most individuals.

- Be complimentary and appreciative, not antagonistic, provoking, obnoxious, rude, or abrasive. The Bible says not to speak evil of a ruler (Acts 23:5) and that a soft word breaks down the hardest resistance (Proverbs 25:15).

- Close with a statement of appreciation, and sincerely and genuinely thank him (for his service, for his consideration of your request, etc.), and then ask him for a response to your letter.

The address for your federal Representative or Senator is:

Name of your Representative
U. S. House of Representatives
Washington, DC, 20515

Name of your Senator
U. S. Senate
Washington, DC, 20510

Because letter-writing does have an effect, many churches now are setting aside a portion of one service a month for their members to write letters. While it is very effective—and relatively easy—to organize a church or home letter-writing group, there is some preparation which must be done for this type of group activity.

The church leadership may designate one (or several) individuals to research current bills/issues of concern to the Christian community. (There are several groups listed in Appendix A which monitor issues and bills of importance to Christians; it is beneficial to get on mailing lists of one or all of these groups in order to be informed about current issues.) The church then provides information on these bills or issues to the congregation in conjunction with a service (perhaps on a blackboard, an overhead, or a handout) and next provides the members with the paper and the time necessary to jot a short note to their Congressmen on one of the bills/issues. This entire process usually requires only 10-15 minutes; and since twenty letters can have substantial impact, virtually any church, Sunday School class, home-meeting group, etc. should easily be able to generate more than enough letters on a single bill/issue to create a "crisis" for a Congressman.

Although letters are more effective than calls, calls are still very effective. If you decide to call instead of write, dial the Capitol switchboard at (202) 224-3121. When the operator answers, ask for your Senator or Representative by name. When that office answers, ask to speak to your Congressman. If he is available, often he will speak with you. If he is unavailable, simply express to his staff your concern or how you expect him to vote on a particular issue. The staff *will* record your feelings and *will* communicate them to the Congressman. (This process is just as effective with your state and local leaders as it is with your federal officials.) *Item #7—Become active in communicating with your elected officials.*

•   •   •

[8] Often, we seem to be overwhelmed with bad news and regular reports concerning the loss or compromise of yet another moral or Biblical principle. Why is this the case? According to a recent study, the majority of those working in certain areas of the public media consider themselves "liberal" and support immoral stands which most Godly individuals oppose. [20] We therefore receive a steady presentation of what the "liberal" media believes to be important and a suppression of what we believe to be important. Consequently, we often feel that we are a minority and have no power to alter the stand of our government.

Song of Solomon 8:13 tells us otherwise; it declares a simple principle: "Your companions hearken to your voice, so speak!" You *can* be effective in communicating a different viewpoint to your friends and to others, and one way is through the "Letters to the Editor" section of your local newspaper. Your views can offer an alternative to those frequently presented by the media and can show other silent or discouraged ones that there are many who actually feel as they do. Commit yourself to writing one or two public letters a month.

When composing such a letter, be sure to avoid being purely emotional (and thus often illogical); also, avoid using Christian clichés and phrases—they communicate only to other well-informed Christians and not to the general population. In an English newspaper, you would not write in Japanese, nor would you write in Portuguese; therefore, don't write in Christian-ese. Christian-ese is just as foreign a language to many readers as is Chinese or Swahili. Adopt the philosophy of Paul explained in 1 Corinthians 9:19-22:

> [T]o win as many as possible . . . I became like one under the law so as to win those under the law. To those not having the law I became like one not having the law . . . so as to win those not having the law. To the weak I became weak to win the weak. I have become all things to all men so that by all possible means I might save some.

Utilize the opportunity to give sound, practical reasons for your opinions and to provide a basis for others to adopt your views. As 1 Peter 3:15 instructs: "Be ready to give an answer to everyone." *Item #8— Become informed, then spread that information to others.*

● ● ●

9 As you become more active and involved, don't underestimate the effect of the experience you are gaining. Be willing to step into leadership, perhaps by stepping out to inform the community of important issues and consideration, perhaps by recruiting others to run for office, or perhaps even by running for local offices yourself.

Local offices *are* important—they influence the entire community. Furthermore, it is easier to be elected to local government or to local school boards than to be elected to a statewide or national office. Don't be afraid to run for a position on the local school board, city council, or other areas where you can begin helping to implement changes. While Charles Finney's statement from the mid-1800s is appropriate for every level, it is especially true at the local level:

> Politics are part of a religion in such a country as this and Christians must do their duty to the country as a part of their duty to God. It seems sometimes as if the foundations of the nation are becoming rotten, and Christians seem to act as if they think God does not see what they do in politics.

But I tell you He does see it, and He will bless or curse this nation, according to the course they [Christians] take. [21]

Recognize that involvement in civil government *is* a legitimate ministry: in Luke 19:17-19, Jesus shows that the reward God gave to those who proved themselves faithful was to place them in civil government, and Romans 13:4 declares that civil leaders are "ministers of God." God wants His people in all arenas, including that of government, for government won't be redeemed from without; it must be redeemed from within by people of Godly principles and integrity. *Item #9—Become active in leading community change.*

• • •

10 Finally, it is vital that we develop an attitude of unswervable duty coupled with an attitude of resolute steadfastness. For the most part, our culture has developed a short-term, microwave mentality. Television seems to teach us that a family or a national crisis can arise and be resolved completely within a 30- or 60-minute program; consequently, we have embraced impatience as a national characteristic.

That characteristic too often infects our attitude toward involvement in public affairs. For example, we may get involved in an election or two; but when we don't see a complete turnaround, we have a tendency to throw up our hands, declare that we tried and that it didn't make any difference, then scurry on to our next inspiration. It took nearly half-a-century to arrive at the situation in which we find ourselves today; that situation will not be reversed in one election, or two.

Even if the recovery turns out to be just as lengthy as was the disease, a recovery *will* come *if* we faithfully persist. Galatians 6:9 promises that we will reap the benefits if we will simply hang in there long enough. We must learn to be content with small, steady gains. The principle of retaking lost ground slowly, while neither appealing nor gratifying to our natural impatience, is a well-articulated Biblical principle:

I will *not* drive them out in a single year . . . *Little by little*
I *will* drive them out before you, until you have increased
enough to take possession of the land. EXODUS 23:29-30

The Lord your God *will* drive [them] out before you . . .
little by little. You *will not* be allowed to eliminate them
all at once. DEUTERONOMY 7:22

To retake lost ground quickly is not the strategy prescribed by the
Lord Himself; the rewards promised in the Scriptures go to the *faithful* (Matthew 25:21, 23). Commit yourself to this engagement for
the long haul—for the duration; arm yourself with the mentality of a
marathon runner, not a sprinter. Very simply, be willing to stay and
compete until you win. *Item #10—Develop a long-term resolute spirit.*

——— ——— ——— • • • ——— ——— ———

We must regain the conviction that Biblical principles are vital to
national success, and we must be willing to pursue their reinstate-
ment. In recent decades, we have wrongly allowed the very principles which produced morality and virtue, and thus national stability,
to be restricted in public life. We need once again to recognize the
truth so well understood by George Washington that:

> [T]he propitious [favorable] smiles of Heaven can never
> be expected on a nation that disregards the eternal rules
> of order and right which Heaven itself has ordained. [22]

We must become convinced of the principle expressed by Abraham Lincoln and then accept the civic responsibilities implied by his
statement that:

> The truth announced in the Holy Scripture, and proven
> by all history [is] that, "Those nations *only* are blessed
> whose God is the Lord." [23]

Appendix A
Resource Groups

The following is a list of some of the many organizations helpful for Godly Americans. Most of the groups have newsletters to which one may subscribe (some require a nominal fee; many are free) so that an individual/church/group can become well-informed on many vital issues. Additionally, most of the groups listed in the Pro-Family section, and even some of the Pro-Life and educational groups, have state and local affiliates/chapters and offer voter's guides for federal, state, and often even local candidates.

PRO-FAMILY GROUPS

American Family Association (AFA): Donald E. Wildmon, 107 Parkgate, PO Drawer 2440, Tupelo, MS 38803, 601-844-5036. A Christian organization promoting the Biblical ethics of decency in American society with primary emphasis on TV and other media.

Concerned Women for America (CWA): Beverly LaHaye, 370 L'Enfant Promenade S.W., Suite 800, Washington, D.C. 20024, 202-488-7000. CWA emphasizes both prayer and action, organizing prayer chapters to pray for the nation and its leaders, and providing specific and current information on the status of movements/bills/laws concerning the family.

Eagle Forum: Phyllis Schlafly, Box 618, Alton, IL 62002, 618-462-5415. A group very active in pro-family issues and specializing in educational curriculum content. Their regular publications include "The Phyllis Schlafly Report" and "The Education Reporter." They equip citizen volunteers to be effective influences on governmental policies in federal and state legislatures, and they elect candidates at every level.

Christian Coalition: Ralph Reed, Box 1990, Chesapeake, VA 23320, 804-424-2630. Christian Coalition promotes Christian values through a network of state affiliates and county chapters. It monitors legislative initiatives, interacts with state and local officials, and takes concerted action to further traditional Godly interests. Excellent at training and equipping individuals either to become involved or to run for office.

Focus on the Family: Dr. James Dobson, Colorado Springs, CO 80995, 719-531-3400. A ministry dedicated to strengthening the family by providing information and practical applications on issues ranging from relationships with children to relationships between spouses. Information is provided on social and political issues which have potential impact on the family.

Citizen Magazine: Colorado Springs, CO 91799, 713-531-3400. This branch of "Focus on the Family" has a strong social and practical community focus, and it encourages citizens to apply Christian moral principles to community, state and national issues. It informs citizens about significant issues of national/state interest which justify a letter to the appropriate politician, and it inspires citizens with accounts of average people who have made a difference.

Family Research Council: Dr. Gary Bauer, 601 Pennsylvania Ave., N.W., Suite 901, Washington, D.C. 20004, 202-393-2100. An organization for education, social policy research, and lobbying which publishes monthly newsletters on issues of concern to Godly citizens.

Chinese Family Alliance: Rev. Raymond Kwong, 450 Taraval St. #246, San Francisco, CA 94116, 415-337-1007. The pioneer in the Asian pro-family movement. A non-profit, non-partisan educational organization that seeks to promote community interest and involvement in the preservation of traditional family values and religious liberties.

LEGAL GROUPS

American Center for Law and Justice (ACLJ): Jay Sekulow, 1000 Centerville Turnpike, Virginia Beach, VA 23463, 804-579-2489. A state-by-state network of attorneys willing to stand up for God and decency in the courtrooms. The ACLJ takes the initiative in confronting the humanists, leftists, and the infamous ACLU who have been systematically destroying America's religious and moral foundations.

The National Legal Foundation: PO Box 64845, Virginia Beach, VA 23464, 804-424-4242. A public interest law firm dedicated to the preservation of First Amendment rights, of freedom of religion, speech, assembly, and the press.

The Rutherford Institute: John Whitehead, PO Box 4782, Charlottesville, VA 22906-7482, 804-978-3888. A nonprofit civil liberties organization founded to defend the rights of religious persons and to educate the public on important issues of religious liberty and the sanctity of human life.

American Family Association Law Center: 107 Parkgate Drive, PO Drawer 2440, Tupelo, MS 38803, 601-680-3886. An arm of the AFA ministry which defends Christians whose Constitutionally protected civil rights are under attack.

Christian Legal Society: PO Box 1492, Merifield, VA 22116-1492, 703-642-1070. A network of attorneys helping establish legal principles to safeguard our freedoms, to educate people about those principles, and to help Christians on a case-by-case basis to get the legal assistance that they need.

Christian Law Association: PO Box 30, Conneaut, OH 44030-0030, 216-493-3933; 216-599-8900. A legal ministry of help to Bible-believing churches and Christians.

PRO-LIFE GROUPS

American United for Life: 343 S. Dearborn, Suite 1804, Chicago, IL 60604, 312-786-9494. An educational and legal pro-life group concerned with protecting human life and combatting abortion or euthanasia.

National Right to Life News: 419 7th Street N.W., Suite 500, Washington, D.C. 20004. Published twice monthly with an absolute commitment to hasten the day that legal protection is returned to every person, born and unborn.

ANTI-PORNOGRAPHY GROUPS

Citizens for Community Values: 11175 Reading Rd., Lower Level, Cincinnati, OH 45241, 513-733-5775. A group dedicated to the elimination of pornography and obscenity through law. Has been extremely effective in helping major cities become completely obscenity free.

National Coalition Against Pornography (NCAP): 800 Compton Rd., Suite 9224, Cincinnati, OH 45231, 513-521-6227. Their focus is to eliminate illegal pornography in the form of obscenity, especially child pornography. They educate the public, law-enforcement, government and community leaders through research and case studies. They involve individuals in supporting good legislation regarding this issue.

Children's Legal Foundation (Formerly Citizens for Decency Through Law): 2845 E. Camelback, Suite 740, Phoenix, AZ 85016, 602-381-1322. They strive to protect the innocence of children by fighting child pornography and attempting to prevent pornographic materials from getting into the hands of youth.

EDUCATIONAL GROUPS

Citizens for Educational Freedom: 927 S. Walter Reed Drive, Suite 1, Arlington, VA 22204, 703-486-8311. A coalition of organizations and individuals dedicated to: (1) freedom of parental choice of schools—public or private—without the loss of tax benefits; (2) freedom from excessive governmental regulation and control of schools.

National Association of Christian Educators/Citizens for Excellence in Education (NACE/CEE): Dr. Robert Simonds, Box 3200, Costa Mesa, CA 92628, 714-546-5931. A grassroots Christian ministry dedicated to helping families reform and reshape public school education at the local level and thereby restore academic excellence, Godly morals, and traditional American values to the classroom. They organize local chapters to work with the local school officials.

Christian Educators Association (CEA): Forrest Turpin, PO Box 50025, Pasadena, CA 91105, 818-798-1124. A networking organization whose primary objective is to support Christian educators and equip them with the tools they need to have an indelible influence on America's youth. CEA provides counseling and referral services for specific questions in areas such as curricula, schoolbook policy, and legal rights.

National Council on Bible Curriculum in Public Schools: Elizabeth Ridenour, PO Box 9743, Greensboro, NC 27429, 910-272-3799. A program to bring state-certified, elective Bible courses into public schools—an objective which fully complies with the U. S. Constitution and which is supported by recent Supreme Court rulings.

Released Time Bible Classes: Maury Walker, 7436 Midiron Dr., Fair Oaks, CA 95628, 916-967-3972. A non-denomination religious instruction program for public school children based on traditional religious values. By Supreme Court decisions, with written permission a child can be released from school for up to one hour per week for religious instruction.

HISTORICAL GROUPS

WallBuilders: David Barton, PO Box 397, Aledo, TX 76008, 817-441-6044. A ministry dedicated to the recovery of those portions of American history which have now been removed from contemporary texts. After obtaining original copies of textbooks and works and words of the Founders, the information is then republished and distributed.

Providence Foundation: Stephen McDowell, Mark Beliles, PO Box 6759, Charlottesville, VA, 22906, 804-978-4535. They provide excellent historical information on early American history and education with a strong Biblical emphasis and then train Christians to reform the nation and the world from a worldview that is thoroughly Biblical.

The Foundation for American Christian Education: 2946 25th Ave., San Francisco, CA 94132, 804-488-6601. Dedicated to the recovery and restoration of true American historical information. This group is famous for its *Redbooks* (books filled with photocopies of original American documents showing how the principles of Christianity filled public education and government affairs) and for "The Principle Approach" (the use of the philosophy and the method of education used in America's schools in our earlier years).

STUDENT MINISTRIES

Summit Ministries: PO Box 207, Manitou Springs, CO 80829, 719-685-9103. A Christian leadership training center that helps young people understand how their faith relates to their everyday lives. Through its two-week summer camp program, Summit challenges Christian young people to develop a Biblical worldview and use that worldview to effect positive change in their family, school, community, and country.

The Caleb Campaign: Rt. 4, Box 274, West Frankfort, IL 62896, 618-937-2348. This organization's primary purpose is to provide materials for public school Bible clubs. They also publish *Issues and Answers,* a newspaper offering a conservative look at the topics which interest young people—television, movies, evolution, dating, current events, etc.

Probe Ministries: 1900 Firman Dr., #100, Richardson, TX 75801, 214-480-0204. An organization reclaiming Christian values in Western culture. They offer a Christian perspective on academic and social issues, and their College Prep Seminars prepare high-school seniors and college freshmen for the intellectual and spiritual challenges of the college environment.

Dave Roever and Associates: PO Box 136130, Ft. Worth, TX 76136, 800-873-2839, 817-238-2005. A ministry that revolves around the tragic yet inspirational and humorous testimony of a Vietnam Vet who overcame disaster. Besides videos and cassettes, they also offer many beneficial items for today's students, including a list of students' legal rights on a public school campus.

National Network of Youth Ministries: PO Box 60134, Ft. Worth, TX 76115, 817-447-7526, 619-592-9200 (24 Hours). They coordinate *See You At the Pole* which began in 1989 as a vision of students to pray for their friends, school, and country. Their vision has exploded into a powerful movement around the world, crossing denominational and ethnic barriers.

Campus Crusade for Christ: 100 Sunport Lane, Orlando, FL 32809-7875, 800-444-5335. A ministry dedicated to taking Christ to the Campus. Their U. S. ministries include Athletes in Action, Josh McDowell Ministries, and many other groups reaching out to campuses, families, churches, Hollywood, government, the military, etc.

Student Discipleship Ministries: PO Box 6747, Ft. Worth, TX 76115, 817-2965-6198. They offer instructive seminars in Basic Discipleship, Morals, Evangelism, Family, and Stewardship as well as a variety of other materials to enhance the spiritual life of young people.

Aletheia: PO Drawer 2440, Tupelo, MS 38803, 601-844-5036. A ministry of the American Family Association, Aletheia is a student-led, national high-school club for Christians which assists teens in starting local groups to impact their community for the better.

Reel to Real Ministries: PO Box 4145, Gainesville, FL 32613, 904-371-2466. They have a threefold mission: the production of film and video presentations, "live" multimedia presentations and seminars, and the equipping of a new generation to help fulfill the Great Commission using the latest in 21st Century video technology.

Appendix B
Recommended Reading List

This list of books is useful in reclaiming and reteaching American history and heritage. Some of the books are available through nationwide distributors and thus available through most Christian bookstores (indicated by an asterisk—*); others are available only from the group or organization indicated.

*The Myth of Separation** by David Barton. An examination of the quotes of the Founding Fathers and of Supreme Court rulings which establish that Christian principles were to be the basis for the governing of this nation and its schools. The book shows what our roots were, when and how we left them, and what the results have been. Makes revealing and exciting reading.

*The Bulletproof George Washington: An Account of God's Providential Care** by David Barton. This is a reprint of the story of the 23 year-old George Washington and his role in a prominent battle in the French and Indian War. This account once appeared in most history books from 1800-1932, but is now omitted. The story shows God's direct intervention and miraculous protection in the life of Washington.

The New England Primer: First introduced into American schools in 1690, it was one of the main textbooks of American schools for over 200 years. This is the same book from which the Founders learned valuable lessons about life's priorities. A reprint of the 1777 edition. Order from WallBuilders, PO Box 397, Aledo, TX, 76008, 817-441-6044.

*The Light and the Glory** by Peter Marshall and David Manuel. This is a study of American history from the discovery of the nation under Columbus through the time of the Revolution. Quoting from the book-jacket: "As we look at our nation's history from God's point of view, we begin to have an idea of how much we owe a very few— and how much is still at stake. *The Light and the Glory* reveals our true national heritage and inspires us to stay on God's course as a nation." An excellent book!

America's God and Country: Encyclopedia of Quotations by William J. Federer. This book is an invaluable resource to those wishing to find Biblical, God-centered quotes from Founding Fathers, Presidents, Statesmen, Scientists, Court decisions, etc. Well indexed, and with copious footnotes, it is excellent for use in school reports, newspaper editorials, debates, and essays. Order from FAME Publishing, Inc., 820 S. MacArthur Blvd., Ste. 105-220, Coppell, TX 75019-5574.

The McGuffey Readers by William Holmes McGuffey. Originally printed in 1836, the *McGuffey Readers* sold 122 million copies in their first 75 years. These *Readers* promoted desirable character traits in students through stories stressing honesty, integrity, hard work, truthfulness, respect, kindness, etc. Order from the Moore Foundation, 36211 Sunset View, Washougal, WA 98671, 206-835-5392 or 2736.

The Sower Series by Mott Media. A series of biographies of famous individuals, holding forth their Christian character as a model for youth. Quoting from the books: "Read for yourself . . . from the actual pen of these noted people from world history . . . of their relationship to Jesus Christ . . . and how that relationship affected their decisions . . . and the course of human history!" Featured heroes include (a book about each hero): George Washington, Abraham Lincoln, Robert E. Lee, Abigail Adams, Christopher Columbus, Susanna Wesley, Clara Barton, Francis Scott Key, George Washington Carver, Isaac Newton, the Wright Brothers, and many others.

Faith and Freedom: The Christian Roots of American Liberty by Benjamin Hart. Quoting from the book-jacket: "*Faith and Freedom* systematically shatters the many popular misconceptions about America's history and tells the true story . . . America's Founding Fathers understood that faith and freedom go together, that one cannot survive long without the other . . . *Faith and Freedom* is a dramatic narrative, and contains moving portraits of some of freedom's greatest heroes and martyrs. This volume is packed with crucial information largely omitted from today's American history texts."

Faith of Our Founding Fathers by Tim Lahaye. Quoting from the book-jacket: "Were the men who carved this great nation out of the wilderness and drafted its founding documents God-fearing, Bible-believing Christians? Or, where they enlightenment Deists, Transcendentalists, and Unitarians? . . . This book . . . gives undeniable proof that those who established this country were, indeed, faithful Christians, or they were individuals who held firmly to a distinctively Christian view of what America—and the world—should be."

America's Date With Destiny by Pat Robertson. Quoting from the book-jacket: "From the diary of America itself comes a view of history that has been virtually hidden from generations. . . . The central role of Christian faith and biblical truth in shaping the charters of our original colonies, the curriculum of our original schools and universities, even the Declaration of Independence and the Constitution has been censored from the historic record . . . *America's Dates With Destiny* illuminates twenty-three extraordinary events in our nation's history, each date representing a crossroads in our democracy. . . . Clearly shows us where we have been."

God and Government: A Biblical and Historical Study by Gary DeMar. A three-volume combination textbook/workbook designed for individual, group, church, school, and seminar study. Quoting from the Foreword: "The Bible tells us that where there is no vision there is little, if any, future. A necessary ingredient in establishing a vision is the recognition of historical roots. To Americans this means a return to the Biblical foundation that undergirded early America and that has given form and content to our freedoms . . . Gary DeMar's study begins with the question: 'What does the Bible say about God and government?' From there, he analyzes the entire historical and governmental process according to the teachings of the Bible . . . Americans must again study the nature of their civil government."

America's Providential History by Mark A. Beliles and Stephen K. McDowell. This book is a unique study of history, geography, economics, and government in the light of Biblical truths. Quoting from the book: "The goal of *America's Providential History* is to equip Christians to be able to introduce Biblical principles into the public affairs of America, and every nation in the world, and in so doing bring Godly change through the world." Order from The Providence Foundation, PO Box 6759, Charlottesville, VA 22906, 804-978-4535.

Defending the Declaration by Gary Amos. Quoting from the cover: "In recent years, a number of books ... have tried to show that there was almost no Christian influence on the minds and writings of America's forefathers. This book clearly refutes that notion." Order from The Providence Foundation, PO Box 6759, Charlottesville, VA 22906, 804-978-4535.

Celebrations of a Nation: Early American Holidays by Lucile Johnston. This book is a carefully documented and very readable history of this nation and reminds of the vision and covenants of our Founding Fathers by revealing the happenings behind the establishment of the national holidays of Thanksgiving, The Fourth of July, and George Washington's Birthday. Order from Johnston Bicentennial Foundation, 1701 Governors Drive S.E., Huntsville, AL 35801, 205-534-8252.

Story of Liberty by Charles Coffin. A reprint of an 1879 history textbook. This book covers a time period from the late 12th century to the early 1600's and is a refreshing look at history from a Christian worldview. Order from The Providence Foundation, PO Box 6759, Charlottesville, VA 22906, 804-978-4535.

Sweet Land of Liberty by Charles Coffin. Reprint of an 1876 American history textbook, from a Christian worldview, which covers from the time of Christopher Columbus to the American Revolution. Order from The Providence Foundation, PO Box 6759, Charlottesville, VA 22906, 804-978-4535.

Appendix C
1988 National Merit Program
Semi-Finalists

City, State	Total #	Public	%	Private	%
Birmingham, AL	28	14	50.0	14	50.0
Montgomery, AL	24	7	29.0	17	71.0
Phoenix, AZ	37	25	67.6	12	32.4
Tucson, AZ	41	33	80.5	8	19.5
Little Rock, AR	38	27	71.1	11	28.9
Los Angeles, CA	59	28	47.5	31	52.5
Mountain View, CA	7	3	42.9	4	57.1
Oakland, CA	32	7	21.9	25	78.1
Palo Alto, CA	54	46	85.2	8	14.8
San Diego, CA	69	62	89.9	7	10.1
San Francisco, CA	55	29	52.7	26	47.3
Wilmington, DE	22	10	45.5	12	54.5
District of Columbia	72	3	4.2	69	95.8
Ft. Lauderdale, FL	28	11	39.3	17	60.7
Jacksonville, FL	41	28	68.3	13	31.7
Miami, FL	57	38	66.7	19	33.3
Tampa, FL	52	25	48.1	27	51.9
Winter Park, FL	26	22	84.6	4	15.4
Atlanta, GA	80	38	47.5	42	52.5
Savannah, GA	11	3	27.3	8	72.7
Chicago, IL	77	27	35.1	50	64.9
Ft. Wayne, IN	28	17	60.7	11	39.3
Goshen, IN	5	1	20.0	4	80.0
Indianapolis, IN	50	38	76.0	12	24.0
South Bend, IN	26	18	69.2	8	30.8
Lexington, KY	37	29	78.4	8	21.6
Louisville, KY	76	43	56.6	33	43.4
Baton Rouge, LA	46	33	71.7	13	28.3
New Orleans, LA	93	41	44.1	52	55.9
Shreveport, LA	20	19	95.0	1	5.0
Baltimore, MD	35	15	42.9	20	57.1
Bethesda, MD	81	52	64.2	29	35.8
Andover, MA	35	5	14.3	30	85.7
Boston, MA	21	13	61.9	8	38.1
Concord, MA	14	6	42.9	8	57.1
Danvers, MA	15	0	0.0	15	100.0
Lexington, MA	18	18	100.0	0	0.0
Milton, MA	30	2	6.7	28	93.3

City, State	Total #	Public	%	Private	%
Ann Arbor, MI	58	45	77.6	13	22.4
Birmingham, MI	35	14	40.0	21	60.0
Bloomfield Hills, MI	29	11	37.9	18	62.1
Detroit, MI	12	5	41.7	7	58.3
Farmington Hills, MI	17	10	58.8	7	41.2
Flint, MI	8	6	75.0	2	25.0
Grand Rapids, MI	33	25	75.8	8	24.2
Kalamazoo, MI	14	11	78.6	3	21.4
Redford, MI	10	2	20.0	8	80.0
Minneapolis, MN	31	18	58.1	13	41.9
Rochester, MN	26	21	80.8	5	19.2
Jackson, MS	33	8	24.2	25	75.8
Natchez, MS	8	4	50.0	4	50.0
Kansas City, MO	24	8	33.3	16	66.7
Springfield, MO	22	20	90.9	2	9.1
St. Louis, MO	91	8	8.8	83	91.2
Billings, MT	16	16	100.0	0	0.0
Missoula, MT	9	8	88.9	1	11.1
Lincoln, NE	23	19	82.6	4	17.4
Omaha, NE	36	29	80.6	7	19.4
Concord, NH	21	4	19.0	17	81.0
Exeter, NH	36	0	0.0	36	100.0
Princeton, NJ	27	17	63.0	10	37.0
Albuquerque, NM	60	33	55.0	27	45.0
Bronx, NY	57	27	47.4	30	52.6
Brooklyn, NY	31	7	22.6	24	77.4
Buffalo, NY	18	8	44.4	10	55.6
New York, NY	213	138	64.8	75	35.2
Rochester, NY	41	30	73.2	11	26.8
Syracuse, NY	10	9	90.0	1	10.0
Asheville, NC	15	12	80.0	3	20.0
Charlotte, NC	48	35	72.9	13	27.1
Durham, NC	109	101	92.7	8	7.3
Greensboro, NC	21	19	90.5	2	9.5
Raleigh, NC	48	41	85.4	7	14.6
Winston-Salem, NC	28	22	78.6	6	21.4
Akron, OH	17	11	64.7	6	35.3
Cincinnati, OH	120	57	47.5	63	52.5
Cleveland, OH	19	5	26.3	14	73.7
Columbus, OH	37	24	64.9	13	35.1
Toledo, OH	40	11	27.5	29	72.5
Oklahoma City, OK	31	26	83.9	5	16.1
Tulsa, OK	53	29	54.7	24	45.3

City, State	Total #	Public	%	Private	%
Beaverton, OR	18	18	100.0	0	0.0
Portland, OR	35	25	71.4	10	28.6
Bethlehem, PA	13	8	61.5	5	38.5
Erie, PA	8	5	62.5	3	37.5
Lancaster, PA	10	8	80.0	2	20.0
Philadelphia, PA	61	21	34.4	40	65.6
Pittsburgh, PA	78	59	75.6	19	24.4
Providence, RI	22	9	40.9	13	59.1
Columbia, SC	44	42	95.5	2	4.5
Greenville, SC	12	6	50.0	6	50.0
Spartanburg, SC	23	18	78.3	5	21.7
Sioux Falls, SD	13	10	76.9	3	23.1
Chatanooga, TN	19	3	15.8	16	84.2
Knoxville, TN	32	22	68.8	10	31.2
Memphis, TN	63	27	42.9	36	57.1
Nashville, TN	36	14	38.9	22	61.1
Austin, TX	73	67	91.8	6	8.2
Dallas, TX	72	32	44.4	40	55.6
Ft. Worth, TX	29	17	58.6	12	41.4
Houston, TX	157	122	77.7	35	22.3
San Antonio, TX	80	72	90.0	8	10.0
Ogden, UT	2	2	100.0	0	0.0
Provo, UT	18	14	77.8	4	22.2
Salt Lake City, UT	41	39	95.1	2	4.9
Alexandria, VA	46	41	89.1	5	10.9
Arlington, VA	20	18	90.0	2	10.0
Fairfax, VA	35	32	91.4	3	8.6
Richmond, VA	20	13	65.0	7	35.0
Virginia Beach, VA	14	13	92.9	1	7.1
Bellvue, WA	15	13	86.7	2	13.3
Seattle, WA	87	59	67.8	28	32.2
Spokane, WA	24	19	79.2	5	20.8
Tacoma, WA	16	10	62.5	6	37.5
Charleston, WV	16	14	87.5	2	12.5
Parkersburg, WV	19	16	84.2	3	15.8
Madison, WI	37	35	94.6	2	5.4
Milwaukee, WI	36	13	36.1	23	63.9
Totals	4519	2746	60.8	1773	39.2

Endnotes

Preface

1. *Wallace v. Jaffree*, 105 F. 2d 1526, 1534 (11th Cir. 1983); *Wallace v. Jaffree*, 472 U.S. 37, 44 n. 22 (1985); *Jager v. Douglas*, 862 F. 2d 824 (11th Cir. 1989), cert. denied, 490 U.S. 1090 (1989); *Lundberg v. West Monona Community School District*, 731 F. Supp. 331, 342 (N.D. Iowa 1989); *Graham v. Central Community School District of Decatur County*, 608 F. Supp. 531, 535 (D.C. Iowa 1985); *Walter v. West Virginia Bd. of Educ.*, 610 F. Supp. 1169, 1176 n. 5 (D.C.W.Va. 1985); *Duffy v. Las Cruces Public Schools*, 557 F. Supp. 1013, 1019 (D.C.N.M. 1983); *United Christian Scientists v. Christian Science Board of Directors, First Church of Christ, Scientist*, 829 F. 2d 1152, 1166 (D.C. Cir. 1987); *Karen B. v. Treen*, 653 F. 2d 897, 901 (5th Cir. 1981), 455 U.S. 913, affirmed; *Weisman v. Lee*, 908 F. 2d 1090, 1097 (1st Cir. 1990); plus others.

Chapter 1: A Historical Overview

1. *Compton's Pictured Encyclopedia and Fact Index* (Chicago: F. E. Compton & Company, 1954), "The Story of Christianity," Vol. 3, p. 301.
2. John W. Whitehead, *The Separation Illusion: A Lawyer Examines the First Amendment* (Milford, MI: Mott Media, 1977), p. 18.
3. Noah Webster, *The Letters of Noah Webster*, Harry A. Warfel, ed. (New York: Library Press, 1953), p. 453, to David McClure on October 25, 1836.
4. Benjamin Rush, *Essays, Literary, Moral and Philosophical* (Philadelphia: Thomas and William Bradford, 1806), p. 8. From his "Of the Mode of Education Proper in a Republic."
5. Benjamin Rush, *Letters of Benjamin Rush*, L. H. Butterfield, editor (Princeton: Princeton University Press, 1951), Vol. I, p. 294, to John Armstrong on March 19, 1783.
6. James Madison, *The Papers of James Madison* (Washington: Langtree & O'Sullivan, 1840), Vol. II, pp. 984-986.
7. *Supra* note 5 at Vol. I, p. 475, to Elias Boudinot on July 9, 1788.
8. James D. Richardson, *A Compilation of the Messages and Papers of the Presidents, 1789-1897* (Published by Authority of Congress, 1899), Vol. 1, pp. 52.
9. *Id.* at Vol. 1, p. 53.
10. George Washington, *Address of George Washington, President of the United States, and Late Commander in Chief of the American Army, to the People of the United States, Preparatory to His Declination* (Baltimore: George and Henry S. Keatinge, Booksellers, 1796), pp. 22-23.

Chapter 2: 1962—A New Direction For America

1. *Engel v. Vitale;* 370 U.S. 421, 425 (1962).
2. *School Dist. of Abington Township v. Schempp;* 374 U.S. 203 (1963).
3. *Stone v. Graham;* 449 U.S. 39, 42 (1980).
4. *Graham v. Central Community School District of Decatur County;* 608 F. Supp. 531, 536 (W.D.N.Y. 1985).
5. *Kay by Disselbrett v. Douglas School District;* 719 F. 2d 875 (Or.Ct.App. 1986).
6. *Jager v. Douglas;* 862 F. 2d 824, 825 (11th Cir. 1989).
7. *Lee v. Weisman;* 120 L. Ed. 2d 467 (1992).

8. *Stein* v. *Oshinsky;* 348 F. 2d 999 (2nd Cir. 1965), cert. denied, 382 U.S. 957.

9. *Collins* v. *Chandler Unified School District;* 644 F. 2d 759, 760 (9th Cir. 1981), cert. denied, 454 U.S. 863.

10. *Reed* v. *Van Hoven;* 237 F. Supp. 48 (W.D. Mich. 1965).

11. *State of Ohio* v. *Whisner;* 351 N.E. 2d 750 (Ohio Sup. Ct. 1976).

12. John Eidsmoe, *Christianity and the Constitution* (Grand Rapids, MI: Baker Book House, 1987), p. 406.

13. William J. Murray, "America Without God," *The New American,* June 20, 1988, p. 19.

14. "Parent Silences Teaching of Carols," *Washington Times,* Dec. 12, 1988.

15. Stephen K. McDowell and Mark A. Beliles, *America's Providential History* (Charlottesville, VA: Providence Press, 1988), p. 79.

16. *Walz* v. *Tax Commission;* 397 U.S. 664, 702 (1970), Douglas, J., dissenting (emphasis added).

17. *School Dist. of Abington Township* v. *Schempp;* 374 U.S. 203, 220-221 (1963) (emphasis added).

18. Lawrence A. Cremin, *1963 Yearbook, World Book Encyclopedia,* p. 38 (emphasis added).

19. Richard L. Worsnop, "Supreme Court: Legal Storm Center," *Editorial Research Reports,* Sept. 28, 1966, pp. 707-708 (emphasis added).

20. *Zorach* v. *Clauson;* 343 U.S. 306, 312 (1952).

21. *City of Charleston* v. *S. A. Benjamin;* 2 Strob. 508, 520, 523 (S.C. Sup. Ct. 1846).

22. *People* v. *Ruggles;* 8 Johns 470, 545-546 (N.Y. Sup. Ct. 1811).

23. *Wallace* v. *Jaffree,* 105 F. 2d 1526, 1534 (11th Cir. 1983); *Wallace* v. *Jaffree,* 472 U.S. 37, 44 n. 22 (1985); *Jager* v. *Douglas,* 862 F. 2d 824 (11th Cir. 1989), cert. denied, 490 U.S. 1090 (1989); *Lundberg* v. *West Monona Community School District,* 731 F. Supp. 331, 342 (N.D. Iowa 1989); *Graham* v. *Central Community School District of Decatur County,* 608 F. Supp. 531, 535 (D.C. Iowa 1985); *Walter* v. *West Virginia Bd. of Educ.,* 610 F. Supp. 1169, 1176 n. 5 (D.C.W.Va. 1985); *Duffy* v. *Las Cruces Public Schools,* 557 F. Supp. 1013, 1019 (D.C.N.M. 1983); *United Christian Scientists* v. *Christian Science Board of Directors, First Church of Christ, Scientist,* 829 F. 2d 1152, 1166 (D.C. Cir. 1987); *Karen B.* v. *Treen,* 653 F. 2d 897, 901 (5th Cir. 1981), 455 U.S. 913, affirmed; *Weisman* v. *Lee,* 908 F. 2d 1090, 1097 (1st Cir. 1990); plus others.

24. *Engel* v. *Vitale;* 370 U.S. 421, 422 (1962).

Chapter 3: "Us"—The Youth

1. George Washington, *Address of George Washington, President of the United States, and Late Commander in Chief of the American Army, to the People of the United States, Preparatory to His Declination* (Baltimore: George and Henry S. Keatinge, Booksellers, 1796), p. 23.

2. *Kendrick* v. *Bowen;* 657 F. Supp. 1547, 1562, 1563, 1564, 1565 (D.D.C. 1987).

3. California Coalition for Traditional Values, "California Voter's Guide," Vol. 5, No. 10, Fall 1988.

4. Hon. Bill Bradley of the 76th State District of California prepared an informational packet excerpting books recommended by Planned Parenthood; information packet released by Bradley's office on January 15, 1987.

5. Wardell B. Pomeroy, Ph.D., *Boys and Sex* (NY: Delacorte Press, 1981).

6. Wardell B. Pomeroy, Ph.D., *Girls and Sex* (NY: Delacorte Press, 1981).

7. Rocky Mountain Planned Parenthood, *You've Changed the Combination* (Denver: RAJ Publications, 1977).

8. Pointed Publications, *The Great Orgasm Robbery* (Lakewood, CO: RAJ Publications, 1981), p. 15.

9. *Davis v. Beason;* 133 U.S. 333, 343 (1890).

10. Percentages calculated from raw data obtained from Department of Health and Human Services and the Center for Disease Control.

11. Alan Guttmacher Institute, "Teenage Pregnancy in Developed Countries," Volume 17, Number 2, March/April 1985.

12. "Social Costs of Teenage Sexuality," *Society*, Vol. 36, No. 6, Sept./Oct. 1993, p. 4.

13. Kathy McCoy, "Sex," *Teen*, December 1992, p. 34.

14. Robert Crooks and Karla Bauer, *Our Sexuality* (Menlo Park, CA.: The Benjamin/ Cummings Publishing Co., 1987), p. 441.

15. Susan McBee, "A Call to Tame the Genie of Teen Sex," *U.S. News & World Report*, December 22, 1986, p. 8.

16. *Supra* note 13.

17. Interview with Josh McDowell over material in his book, *Why Wait?* (San Bernadino, CA: Here's Life Publishers, 1987).

18. *Dallas Times Herald,* July 15, 1988, B-3.

19. Based on information provided by the Community Services Department of the Houston Independent School District in an interview on May 16, 1991.

20. *Supra* note 12.

21. Martha R. Burt, "Estimating the Public Costs of Teenage Childbearing," *Family Planning Perspectives*, Vol. 18, No. 5, Sep/Oct 1986. Supplied by Alan Guttmacher Institute.

22. Congressional Budget Office, Congress of the United States, "Sources of Support For Adolescent Mothers," September 1990, p. 36. The study "Teenage Sexual and Reproductive Behavior in the United States," published by the Alan Guttmacher Institute, 1991, reported the amount as $21 billion.

23. Lindsay van Gelder and Pam Brandt, "Teenage Pregnancy: The Crisis in America," *McCalls*, May 1987, p. 83.

24. *Id.*

25. *Time*, December 9, 1985, p. 79.

26. Percentages calculated from raw data obtained from Department of Health and Human Services and the Center for Disease Control.

27. *Supra* note 13.

28. *Id.*

29. *Id.*

30. *Id.* at p. 30.

31. *Id.* at p. 32.

32. *Id.* at p. 34.

33. *Id.* at p. 32.

34. *Supra* note 12.

35. *Supra* note 10.

36. *Supra* note 13 at p. 32.

37. *Parade Magazine*, December 18, 1988, p. 8.

38. *MS Magazine*, July 1983, p. 40.

39. *Supra* note 13.

40. *Parade Magazine*, December 18, 1988, p. 8. See also Susan McBee, "A Call to Tame the Genie of Teen Sex," *U.S. News & World Report*, December 22, 1986, p. 8.

41. *Supra* note 17.

42. U. S. Department of Education review of the 1986 Planned Parenthood Poll by Louis Harris and Associates, Inc., published on December 1, 1987, p. 3.

43. Jared Sparks, *The Life of Gouverneur Morris* (Boston: Gray and Bowen, 1832), Vol. III, p. 483.

44. *USA Today*, September 1985. See also *Christian School Comment*, Vol. 19, No. 3.

45. *Id.*

46. William V. Wells, *The Life and Public Services of Samuel Adams* (Boston: Little, Brown, and Co., 1865), Vol. III, p. 327.

47. Noah Webster, *Letters of Noah Webster*, Harry A Warfel, editor (New York: Library Publishers, 1953), pp. 453-454, to David McClure on Oct. 25, 1836.

48. Benjamin Rush, *Essays, Literary, Moral, and Philosophical* (Philadelphia: Thomas and William Bradford, 1806), p. 8.

49. *Id.* at p. 112.

50. Benjamin Rush, *Letters of Benjamin Rush*, L. H. Butterfield, editor (Princeton: Princeton University Press, 1951), Vol. I, p. 294, to John Armstrong on March 19, 1783.

51. Daniel Webster, *The Works of Daniel Webster* (Boston: Little, Brown, and Company, 1853), Vol. I, pp. 41-42, December 22, 1820.

52. *Id.* at Vol. II, pp. 107-108, October 5, 1840.

53. *Id.* at Vol. II, p. 615, July 4, 1851.

54. John Quincy Adams, *Letters of John Quincy Adams to His Son on the Bible and Its Teachings* (Auburn: James M. Alden, 1850), p. 62.

55. *Age-Specific Arrest Rate and Race-Specific Arrest Rates for Selected Offenses, 1965-1992* (U. S. Department of Justice, Federal Bureau of Investigation, 1993), pp. 45-49.

56. *Id.* at 21-25.

57. *Id.* at 13-17.

58. *Id.* at 29-33.

59. Study by the Rhode Island Rape Crisis Center released through the *Providence Journal-Bulletin*, May 1, 1988 (emphasis added).

60. *Id.*

61. *Id.* at Section A, p. 1.

62. *Hearings Before the Subcommittee on Constitutional Amendments of the Committee on the Judiciary. United States Senate, Eighty-Ninth Congress, Second Session on Senate Joint Resolution 148. Relating to Prayer in Public Schools. August 1, 2, 3, 4, 5, 8, 1966* (Washington: U. S. Government Printing Office, 1966), p. 688, chart 1.

63. Robert Winthrop, *Addresses and Speeches on Various Occasions* (Boston: Little, Brown & Co., 1852), p. 172 from his "Either by the Bible or the Bayonet."

64. *Supra* note 48 at p. 113.

Chapter 4: "Our Parents"—The Family

1. *Grigsby* v. *Reib;* 153 S.W. 1124, 1129-30 (Tex.Sup.Ct. 1913).

2. *Sheffield* v. *Sheffield;* 3 Tex. 79, 85-86 (Tex.Sup.Ct. 1848).

3. Alexander Hamilton, *The Papers of Alexander Hamilton,* Harold C. Syrett, editor (New York: Columbia University Press, 1974), Vol. XXI, pp. 402-404, "The Stand No. III," New York, April 7, 1798.

4. Benjamin Franklin, *The Works of Benjamin Franklin,* Jared Sparks, editor (Boston: Charles Tappan, 1847), Vol. IX, p. 478, to John Sargent on January 27, 1783.

5. George Washington, *The Writings of George Washington from the Original Manuscript Sources, 1745-1799,* John C. Fitzpatrick, editor (Washington: U.S. Government Printing Office, 1938), Vol. XXVIII, p. 514, to Charles Armand-Tuffin on August 10, 1786.

6. James Wilson, *The Works of James Wilson,* Robert Green McCloskey, editor (Cambridge: Belknap Press of the Harvard University Press, 1967), Vol. 2, p. 598, 599, 601, 603.

7. James Kent, *Commentaries on American Law* (New York: Da Capo Press, 1971), an unabridged reproduction of the first edition published in New York between 1826 and 1830), Vol. II, p. 96, 97, 98, 159.

8. Zephaniah Swift, *A System of the Laws of the State of Connecticut* (Windham: Printed by John Byrne, for the Author, 1795), Vol. I, pp. 183, 185, 190, 192.

9. *Commonwealth* v. *Nesbit;* 84 Pa. 398, 406 (Pa.Sup.Ct. 1859).

10. George Washington, *Address of George Washington, President of the United States, and Late Commander in Chief of the American Army, to the People of the United States, Preparatory to His Declination* (Baltimore: George and Henry S. Keatinge, Booksellers, 1796), p. 25.

11. *Supra* note 8 at Vol. I, p. 185.

12. Richard Hettlinger, *Your Sexual Freedom: Letters to Students* (New York: Continuum, 1981), pp. 119-127. See also Gary E. Kelly, *Learning about Sex: The Contemporary Guide for Young Adults* (Woodbury, N.Y.: Baron's Educational Series, Inc., 1986), pp. 130-132, and Robert Crooks, *Our Sexuality* (Menlo Park, CA.: The Benjamin/Cummings Publishing Co., 1987), pp. 471-475.

13. *Journal of Marriage and Family,* Vol. 53, August 1991, p. 669, and *Time,* September 5, 1988, p. 54

14. *USA Today,* September 1989, p. 10.

15. *Psychology Today,* March 1989, p. 77.

16. *Psychology Today,* July/August 1988, p. 15. See also *Demography,* Vol. 26, No. 4, November 1989, p. 621. See also *Social Forces,* September 1990, Vol. 69(1), p. 207.

17. "Runaway Youth: A Profile," *Children Today,* Jan./Feb. 1986, p 4.

18. *Id.*

19. Glenn Collins, "Study Finds That Abuse Causes Children to Flee," *New York Times,* February 10, 1986.

20. *Id.*

21. "Services to Runaways..." *Children Today,* Jan./Feb. 1984, pp. 22-23.

22. *Id.*

23. "Adolescence: No Place Like Home," *Psychology Today,* December 1986, p. 12.

24. "Throwaways," *Ladies Home Journal,* January 1986, p. 44.

25. *Supra* note 19.

26. *Id.*

27. *Supra* note 10.

Chapter 5: "Our Teachers"—American Education

1. U. S. Department of Education, National Center for Education Statistics, *Private School Universe Survey: 1991-92* (Washington, D. C., 1994), p. 4.

2. *Washington Post,* February 3, 1985, p. A-10.

3. National Commission on Excellence in Education, *A Nation at Risk: The Imperative For Educational Reform* (Washington, D. C.: U. S. Government Printing Office, 1983), p. 8 (emphasis added).

4. Phyllis Schlafly, *Child Abuse in the Classroom* (Alton, IL: Marquette Press, 1984), p. 400 (emphasis added).

5. William J. Bennett, Secretary of Education, *American Education—Making It Work* (Washington, D. C.: U. S. Government Printing Office, 1988), p. 13 (emphasis added).

6. National Center for Educational Statistics, Department of Education, *The Condition of Education, 1987* (Washington, D. C.: U. S. Government Printing Office, 1987) p. 145 (emphasis added).

7. *Id.* at pp. 7-8 (emphasis added).

8. *Dallas Times Herald,* December 20, 1983, "The ABC's of Failure," p. 18 A.

9. *Id.* at p. 34 A.

10. *New York Times,* January 4, 1987, Part I, p. 3.

11. *Id.*

12. *Supra* note 8 at Front Page.

13. *Id.* at p. 23.

14. *Id.* at Front Page.

15. *What's Happening in Teacher Testing: An Analysis of State Teacher Testing Practices* (Washington: U. S. Government Printing Office, 1987), p. 45, table 57.

16. *Supra* note 3 at p. 9.

17. *Supra* note 8 at p. 61.

18. *Supra* note 3 at p. 23.

19. *Los Angeles Times,* December 8, 1986, Part I, p. 3.

20. *Fort Worth Star-Telegram,* May 22, 1988, Section I, p. 1.

21. *New York Times,* April 29, 1987, A-1.

22. *Chicago Sun-Times,* January 16, 1991, p. 1, "School arrests hit 4306 in 4 mos.," by Maribeth Vander Weele.

23. *Fort Worth Star-Telegram,* September 9, 1990.

24. "Safe Schools Study," National Institute of Education, 1978.

25. Boston Safe Schools Commission, Violence, Victimization and Discipline in Four Boston Public High Schools, 1983.

26. Information obtained from a joint-study by the National School Safety Center and the Virginia Department of Education.

27. Percentages calculated from published and unpublished statistical data from National Center for Health Statistics and Division of Vital Statistics of the Department of Health and Human Services.

28. Herbert Kohl, "What Teen Suicide Means," *Nation,* May 9, 1987, p. 603. See also *Newsweek,* March 23, 1987, pp. 28-29.

29. *Statistical Abstract of the United States, 1993* (Washington, D. C.: U. S. Bureau of the Census, 1993), p. 93.

30. *Washington Post,* April 21, 1987, Section A, p. 19, "Lost in Geography," by James J. Kilpatrick.

31. Richard J Kopec, *Geography: No "Where" in North Carolina,* Survey of students at University of North Carolina, 1984.

32. *American Education: Making It Work* (Washington: U.S. Government Printing Office, 1988), p. 13, quoting Mark Krug, *The Melting of Ethnics: Education of the Immigrants, 1880-1914* (Bloomington, IN: Phi Delta Kappa Educational Foundation, 1976), p. 87.

33. *The Washington Times,* October 9, 1989, Section A-1, "Reforms sought as college seniors stumble on history and literature," by Joyce Price.   .

34. *Wall Street Journal,* September 28, 1987.

35. *New York Times,* September 3, 1986.

36. *Fort Worth Star Telegram,* January 4, 1988, Section I, p. 3.

37. January 5, 1988; Information provided in interview with author of previously cited article for further analysis.

38. *Dallas Times Herald,* December 14, 1983, "The ABC's of Failure," p. 19.

39. *Wall Street Journal,* September 28, 1987, Section 2, p. 35.

40. Edwin West, *American Education,* Jan/Feb 1984.

41. *New York Times,* July 8, 1986, C-8.

42. *Id.*

43. *Supra* note 3 at pp. 8, 9, 11, 20, 21.

44. James Madison, *The Papers of James Madison* (Washington: Langtree & O'Sullivan, 1840), Vol. II, pp. 984-986.

Chapter 6: "Our Country"—The Nation

1. *Updegraph v. The Commonwealth;* 11 Serg. & R. 393, 402, 403, 406 (Pa.Sup.Ct. 1824).

2. *City of Charleston v. S. A. Benjamin;* 2 Strob. 508, 518, 523 (S.C.Sup.Ct. 1846).

3. *People v. Ruggles;* 8 Johns 545, 546 (N.Y.Sup.Ct. 1811).

4. Tim LaHaye, *Faith of Our Founding Fathers* (Brentwood, TN: Wolgemuth & Hyatt, 1987), p. 15.

5. This information is collected by Cambell University Law School and the Christian Legal Society and is documented in the monthly *Religious Freedom Reporter.*

6. George Washington, *Address of George Washington, President of the United States, and Late Commander in Chief of the American Army, to the People of the United States, Preparatory to His Declination* (Baltimore: George and Henry S. Keatinge, Booksellers, 1796), p. 22-23.

7. Noah Webster, *The History of the United States* (New Haven: Durrie & Peck, 1833), p. 309, ¶ 53 (emphasis added).

8. William Linn, *The Life of Jefferson* (Ithaca: Mack & Andrus, 1834), p. 265.

9. John Quincy Adams, *Letters of John Quincy Adams to His Son on the Bible and Its Teachings* (Auburn: James M. Alden, 1850), p. 61.

10. Daniel Webster, *Works of Webster* (Boston: Little, Brown & Co, 1853), Vol. II, p. 615 on July 4, 1851.

11. John Adams, *The Works of John Adams, Second President of the United States,* Charles Francis Adams, ed. (Boston: Little, Brown & Co., 1854), Vol. IX, p. 229, October 11, 1798.

12. Dorothy Scheuer, "What Crime Costs," *Scholastic Update,* September 30, 1983, pp. 5-6.

13. *Id.*

14. *Id.*

15. *Id.*

16. Increase based on information obtained from the *Statistical Abstract of the United States* from 1962-1993.

17. *City of Charleston* v. *S. A. Benjamin;* 2 Strob. 508, 520, 523 (S.C.Sup.Ct. 1846).

18. See "Sex, with Care," by Lewis J. Lord with Jeannye Thornton, Joseph Carey, and the Domestic Bureaus, *U. S. News & World Report,* June 2, 1986, p. 53.

19. *Id.*

20. See Paul J. Wiesner, M.D., "Magnitude of the Problem of Sexually Transmitted Diseases in the United States," *Sexually Transmitted Diseases—1980 Status Report,* p. 22. Reprinted by the U. S. Department of Health and Human Services, Public Health Service.

21. See "A Nasty New Epidemic—Concern is growing over sexually transmitted diseases," by Jean Seligmann with George Raine in San Francisco, Vincent Coppola in Atlanta, Mary Hager in Washington, Mariana Gosnell in New York and bureau reports, *Newsweek,* Feb. 4, 1985, p. 73.

22. See "Genital Herpes Infection—1966-1984," U. S. Department of Health and Human Services Public Health Service, *MMWR,* June 20, 1986, Vol. 35, No. 24, pp. 402-404.

23. *Supra* note 21.

24. See "Trends in Molluscum Contagiosum in the United States, 1966-1983," by Thomas M. Becker, M.D., Joseph H. Blount, M.P.H., John Douglas, M.D., and Franklyn N. Judson, M.D., *Sexually Transmitted Diseases,* Apr./Jun. 1986, Vol. 13, No. 2, pp. 88-92, U. S. Department of Health and Human Services, Public Health Service.

25. *Supra* note 20 at p. 23.

26. "Social Costs of Teenage Sexuality," *Society,* Vol. 36, No. 6, Sept./Oct. 1993, p. 4.

27. *Supra* note 21.

28. *Id.* at p. 73.

29. *Id.*

30. *Id.*

31. *Id.*

32. *Id.*

33. Sara Nelson, "A Nation Under the Influence," *Seventeen,* March 1990, p. 183.

34. Statistics obtained from the U. S. Department of Justice, updated annually in *Crime in the United States.*

35. Richard A. Hawley, "School Children and Drugs: The Fancy That Has Not Passed," *Phi Delta Kappan,* May 1987, p. K1.

36. *Supra* note 33.

37. *Supra* note 35.

38. *The Almanac of the Christian World, 1991-1992* (Wheaton, IL: Tyndale House Publishers, 1991), p. 479.

39. *Supra* note 33.

40. *Id.*

41. *Id.*

42. Donato Alvarez and Brian Cooper, "Productivity trends in manufacturing in the U.S. and 11 other countries," *Monthly Labor Review,* January 1984, Vol. 107, pp. 56-57, U. S. Labor Dept. Statistics Bureau.

43. Martin Neil Baily, "What Has Happened to Productivity Growth?" *Science,* Oct. 24, 1986, Vol. 234, p. 443. Information referenced from Department of Labor, Bureau of Labor Statistics, *Productivity Indexes for Selected Industries, 1979 Edition* (Washington, D. C.: U. S. Government Printing Office, 1979), p. 2.

44. *Supra* note 6 at pp. 23-24.

45. Benjamin Franklin, *The Works of Benjamin Franklin,* John Bigelow, editor (New York: G.P. Putnam's Sons, 1904), Vol. XI, pp. 297-298, to Thomas Paine.

Chapter 7: The Emergence of New National Problems

1. "America on Drugs," *U. S. News & World Report,* July 28, 1986, p. 48.

2. *Safe Schools Overview,* National School Safety Center.

3. Richard A. Hawley, "School Children and Drugs: The Fancy That Has Not Passed," *Phi Delta Kappan,* May 1987, p. K1.

4. Fred M. Hechinger, "Concern Over Schooling of Military Recruits," *New York Times,* July 8, 1986.

5. *Supra* note 2.

6. *Id.*

7. "The Drug Sources Must be Stopped," University of Michigan Survey, *Reader's Digest,* August 1983, p. 138.

8. *Education Week,* June 13, 1985, p. 28.

9. *Id.*

10. *Id.*

11. Janice C. Simpson, "A Shallow Labor Pool Spurs Businesses to Act to Bolster Education," *Wall Street Journal,* September 28, 1987.

12. Texas Literacy Council, *Developing Human Capital,* p. 2, 1991.

Chapter 8: National Accountability and Biblical Repercussions

1. *The Constitutions of the Several Independent States of America* (Boston: Norman and Bowen, 1785), p. 81, Pennsylvania Frame of Government, Sec. 10.

2. *Statutes of the State of Vermont* (Vermont: Anthony Haswell, 1791), p. 9.

3. *Supra* note 1 at p. 146, Sec. 13.

4. *The American's Guide: The Constitutions of the United States of America* (Trenton: Moore and Lake, 1813), p. 342, Art. VIII, Sec. II.

5. See Matt. 25: 31-46; II Cor. 5:10; Rom. 14:10; Heb. 9:27; Rev. 20:13.

6. James Madison, *The Papers of James Madison* (Washington: Langtree & O'Sullivan,

1840), Vol. III, pp. 1391.

7. *Id.* at Vol. II, pp. 984-985.

8. Thomas Jefferson, *Notes on the State of Virginia* (Philadelphia: Mathew Carey, 1794), Query XVIII, p. 237.

9. *Abraham Lincoln's Stories and Speeches,* J. B. McClure, editor (Chicago: Rhodes & McClure Pub. Co., 1896), pp. 185-186; John Wesley Hill, *Abraham Lincoln—Man of God* (New York, G. P. Putnam's Sons, 1920), p. 330.

10. *A Nation at Risk: The Imperative for Education Reform* (Washington: U. S. Government Printing Office, 1983), p. 5

11. Information provided by Bankruptcy Division, Administrative Office of the U. S. Courts, Washington, D. C.

12. *Supra* note 6 at Vol. II, p. 985.

Chapter 9: Strategy For a Change

1. *Abington* v. *Schempp,* 374 U.S. 203, 213 (1963).

2. *The Constitutions of the Several Independent States of America* (Boston: Norman and Bowen, 1785), p. 99-100, Sec. 22.

3. *Id. at* p. 81, Pennsylvania Frame of Government, Sec. 10.

4. *Id. at* p. 31, Chapter VI, Article I of Massachusetts Constitution.

5. *Church of the Holy Trinity* v. *United States;* 143 U.S. 457 (1892).

6. Steve C. Dawson, *God's Providence in America's History* (Rancho Cordova, CA: Steve C. Dawson, 1988), p. 11:7.

Chapter 10: What Can Be Done Now?

1. Thomas Clarkson, *Memoirs of the Private and Public Life of William Penn* (London: Longman, Hunt, Rees, Orme, and Brown, 1813), Vol. I, p. 303.

2. *The Unchurched American . . . 10 Years Later* (Princeton: The Princeton Religion Research Center, 1988), p. 25.

3. *Religion in America: 92-93* (Princeton: The Princeton Religion Research Center), p. 20, from a survey conducted for the Christian Broadcasting Network, Inc., by The Gallup Organization, Inc., in 1986.

4. D. Gilbert, *Compendium of American Public Opinion* (New York: Facts on File Publications, 1988), p. 313.

5. *Congressional Record,* June 29, 1987, H. 3511, citing *General Social Survey Annual* of the National Opinion Research Center.

6. U. S. House of Representatives, *What America Believes: The Rest of the Story* (Republican Staff of the Select Committee on Children, Youth, and Families, U. S. House of Representatives, 1990), p. 12, citing the *Boston Globe,* October 31, 1989.

7. John M. Taylor, *Garfield of Ohio: The Available Man* (New York: W. W. Norton and Company, Inc.), p. 180. Quoted from "A Century of Progress," by James A. Garfield, published in *Atlantic,* July 1877.

8. John Bartlett, *Familiar Quotations* (Boston: Little, Brown & Co., 1980), p. 374.

9. John Jay, *The Correspondence and Public Papers of John Jay, 1794-1826,* Henry P. Johnston, editor (New York: G. P. Putnam's Sons, 1893), Vol. IV, p. 365.

10. *Id.* at Vol. IV, p. 393.

11. Daniel Webster, *The Works of Daniel Webster* (Boston: Little, Brown and Company, 1853), Vol. II, p. 108, on October 5, 1840.

12. Noah Webster, *The History of the United States* (New Haven: Durrie and Peck, 1832), pp. 336-337, ¶49.

13. Charles G. Finney, *Revival Lectures* (Old Tappan, NJ: Fleming Revell Co., reprinted 1970), Lecture XV, pp. 336-337.

14. M. L. Weems, *The Life of Washington* (Philadelphia: Joseph Allen, 1800), pp. 6-7..

15. Elias Boudinot, *An Oration, Delivered at Elizabeth-town, New-Jersey... on the Fourth of July* (Elizabethtown: Kollock, 1793), pp. 14-15.

16. John Adams, *The Works of John Adams, Second President of the United States* (Boston: Charles C. Little and James Brown, 1851), Vol. III, p. 437, on August 29, 1763.

17. Alexis De Tocqueville, *The Republic of the United States of America* (New York: A. S. Barnes & Co., 1851), p. 331.

18. Matthias Burnet, D.D., Pastor of the First Church in Norwalk, *An Election Sermon, Preached at Hartford Anniversary Election, May 12, 1803* (Hartford: Hudson and Goodwin, 1803), pp. 26-27.

19. David Ramsay, *An Eulogium Upon Benjamin Rush, M.D.* (Philadelphia: Bradford and Inskeep, 1813), p. 103.

20. S. Robert Lichter and Stanley Rothman, *The Media Elite* (Bethesda, MD: Adler & Adler, 1986), pp. 28-29.

21. Charles G. Finney, *Revival Lectures* (Reprinted Old Tappan, NJ: Fleming Revel Company, 1970), Lecture XV, pp. 336-337.

22. James D. Richardson, *A Compilation of the Message and Papers of the Presidents, 1789-1897* (Published by Authority of Congress, 1899), Vol. I, pp. 52-53.

23. *Id.* at Vol. VI, p. 164, March 30, 1863.

Price List

WallBuilders, Inc.
P.O. Box 397
Aledo, TX 76008
(817) 441-6044

Prices subject to change without notice
Quantity and case-lot discounts available

Books

America: To Pray or Not To Pray?

A statistical look at what has happened when religious principles were separated from public affairs by the Supreme Court in 1962.

The Myth of Separation

An examination of the writings of the Framers of the Constitution and of the Supreme Court's own records concerning the proper role of religious principles in society.

The Bulletproof George Washington

An account of God's miraculous protection of Washington in the French and Indian War and of Washington's open gratitude for God's Divine intervention.

The New England Primer

A reprint of the 1777 textbook used by the Founding Fathers. It was the first textbook printed in America (1690) and was used for 200 years to teach reading and Bible lessons in school.

Noah Webster's "Advice to the Young"

Founder Noah Webster stated that this work "will be useful in enlightening the minds of youth in religious and moral principles and serve to restrain some of the common vices of our country." These timeless lessons are still invaluable for today's youth.

Bible Study Course—New Testament

A reprint of the 1946 New Testament survey text used by the Dallas Public High Schools.

What Happened in Education?

Statistical evidence that disproves several popular educational explanations for the decline in SAT scores.

Did Television Cause the Changes in Youth Morality?

This exam is very enlightening not only as to what happened in television, but when it happened, and why?

Video Cassette (VHS)

America's Godly Heritage (60 min.)

This clearly sets forth the beliefs of many of the famous Founding Fathers concerning the proper role of Christian principles in education, government, and the public affairs of the nation.

Keys to Good Government (59 min.)

Presents the beliefs of the Founders concerning the proper role of Biblically thinking principles in education government, and public affairs.

Education and the Founding Fathers (60 min.)

A look at the Bible-based educational system which produced America's great heroes. It is excellent for learning what was intended by the Founders for America's schools.

Spirit of the American Revolution (53 min.)

A look at the motivation which caused the Founders to pledge their "lives, fortunes, and sacred honor" to establish our new nation.

Foundations of American Government (25 min.)

Surveys the historical statements and records surrounding the drafting of the First Amendment, showing the Founders's intent.

Video Transcripts
America's Godly Heritage (See video)
Education and the Founding Fathers (See video)
Foundations of American Government (See video)
Keys to Good Government (See video)
Spirit of the American Revolution (See video)

Audio Cassette Tapes
Religion & Morality, Indispensable Supports
This tape documents the statements of many Founding Fathers who agreed with Washington that religion and morality are indispensable supports for American society.

Thinking Biblically, Speaking Secularly
Provides guidelines for Biblically thinking individuals to effectively communicate important truths in today's often anti-Biblical environment.

The Founding Fathers
Highlights accomplishments and notable quotes of prominent Founding Fathers which show their strong belief in Christian principles.

The Laws of the Heavens
An explanation of the eight words in the Declaration of Independence on which the nation was birthed.

America: Lessons from Nehemiah
A look at the Scriptural parallels between the rebuilding of Jerusalem in the book of Nehemiah and that of America today.

8 Principles for Reformation
Eight Biblical guidelines for restoring Christian principles to society and public affairs.

America's Godly Heritage (See video)
Keys to Good Government (See video)
Education and the Founding Fathers (See video)
The Spirit of the American Revolution (See video)
Foundations of American Government (See video)
The Myth of Separation (See book)
America: To Pray or Not To Pray (See book)

"Great Americans" Poster Series
Because of the growing interest in restoring our true history and documenting the lives and philosophies of prominent Americans, WallBuilders offers a series of posters designed to give an enjoyable overview of great men and women in America's history (George Washington, Pocahontas, Abraham Lincoln, George Washington Carver, and Thomas Jefferson). These beautiful 16 x 20 informational posters are excellent for use in public, Christian, or home schools.

Pamphlets
The Truth About Thomas Jefferson and the First Amendment
For the past three decades, Thomas Jefferson has often been pointed to as *the* authority on the First Amendment, yet for 170 years prior, he was rarely cited in conjunction with that Amendment. This pamphlet explains the common misconception concerning Jefferson's role with the First Amendment and turns us to the men who did have an influence on it—men such as George Washington, Gouverneur Morris, and Fisher Ames.

Title	Stock#	Price	Quantity	Tot.
Books				
America: To Pray or Not to Pray	(B01)	$6.95	_____	_____
The Myth of Separation	(B02)	$7.95	_____	_____
The Bulletproof George Washington	(B05)	$4.95	_____	_____
The New England Primer	(B06)	$5.95	_____	_____
Noah Webster's "Advice to the Young"	(B10)	$4.95	_____	_____
New Testament Bible Study—Dallas H.S.	(B09)	$4.95	_____	_____
What Happened in Education?	(B03)	$2.95	_____	_____
Did TV Cause the Changes in Youth Morality?	(B04)	$2.95	_____	_____
Video Cassette (VHS)				
America's Godly Heritage	(V01)	$19.95	_____	_____
Keys to Good Government	(V05)	$19.95	_____	_____
Education and the Founding Fathers	(V02)	$19.95	_____	_____
Spirit of the American Revolution	(V04)	$19.95	_____	_____
Foundations of American Government	(V03)	$ 9.95	_____	_____
Video Transcripts				
America's Godly Heritage	(TSC01)	$2.95	_____	_____
Education and the Founding Fathers	(TSC02)	$2.95	_____	_____
Foundations of American Government	(TSC03)	$2.95	_____	_____
Keys to Good Government	(TSC04)	$2.95	_____	_____
Spirit of the American Revolution	(TSC05)	$2.95	_____	_____
Audio Cassette Tapes				
Religion & Morality, Indispensable Supports	(A14)	$4.95	_____	_____
Thinking Biblically, Speaking Secularly	(A13)	$4.95	_____	_____
The Founding Fathers	(A11)	$4.95	_____	_____
The Laws of the Heavens	(A03)	$4.95	_____	_____
America: Lessons from Nehemiah	(A05)	$4.95	_____	_____
8 Principles for Reformation	(A10)	$4.95	_____	_____
America's Godly Heritage	(A01)	$4.95	_____	_____
Keys to Good Government	(A09)	$4.95	_____	_____
Education and the Founding Fathers	(A08)	$4.95	_____	_____
The Spirit of the American Revolution	(A02)	$4.95	_____	_____
Foundations of American Government	(A12)	$4.95	_____	_____
The Myth of Separation	(A06)	$4.95	_____	_____
America: To Pray or Not to Pray	(A07)	$4.95	_____	_____
Great Americans Poster Series				
Poster Set (5 posters)	(P01)	$19.95	_____	_____
George Washington Carver	(P02)	$ 4.95	_____	_____
Thomas Jefferson	(P03)	$ 4.95	_____	_____
Abraham Lincoln	(P04)	$ 4.95	_____	_____
Pocahontas	(P05)	$ 4.95	_____	_____
George Washington	(P06)	$ 4.95	_____	_____
Pamphlets				
Thomas Jefferson and the First Amendment	(PAM01)	$ .50	_____	_____

* When shipping products to multiple addresses, please calculate shipping cost based on the dollar amount to each address—not on the order total. Thank you.

Please allow 4-6 Weeks for delivery.

WallBuilders, PO Box 397, Aledo, TX 76008

SubTotal: _____
Tax (TX only, add 7.75%): _____
Shipping (see chart below): _____
TOTAL: _____

Canada orders add $5 extra.

Under $5.00. . . . $2.00	$25.01-$ 40.00 . . $6.4
$ 5.01-$15.00 . . $3.45	$40.01-$ 60.00 . . $7.4
$15.01-$25.00 . . $4.45	$60.01-$140.00 . . $9.9
	Over $140 7%